Cash Flow Strategies

Cash Flow Strategies

Learn to start a business and make money investing in real estate, factoring notes, and other debt instruments.

Haris Saidi and Trena Saidi

2007

Cash Flow Strategies

Table of Contents

I would like to thank my wife/co-author, Trena, with all the help, input, and support she provided throughout this entire process. I want to also thank the staff at Booksurge for making this book a reality. And last but not least, Fred at www.goliathgraffix.com for designing a wonderful cover.

Members only Website

By purchasing this book you have free access to the members area of this book's website. Simply go to www.cashflowthebook.com and click on Members. Login using username: "member", and password: "cashflow". You will have access to PDF downloads of the following items which will give you the basic foundation to start marketing and branding your business.

- Glossary of Terms
- Business Card Samples
- Sample Newspaper Ads to help grow your business
- Sample business brochures to help give your company a professional image
- Sample flyers to advertise your services
- Sample Postcards to help your marketing efforts via mail
- Sample Press Releases
- Sample Marketing Letters
- Sample Telephone Scripts
- And much more

Introduction overview

In today's financial business world, there exist myriad possibilities for entrepreneurs like you to develop successful businesses. We designed this book to take the core material in a number of different cash flow investing arenas and present it clearly for you to use as a reference guide.

The chapters will go over the most important material on each topic to give you an easy-access book you can turn to when you have questions in your business dealings. We do not intend this book to be an all-encompassing training device on any one topic; rather, we designed it to provide information on many topics, giving you a "one-stop" reference guide.

In the simplest of terms, cash flow investing is buying something for less than the asking price and then selling it (or holding it) for a profit. You can apply it to any financial transaction from merchandise and services to real estate and corporate invoices.

The opportunities for investing this way are increasing dramatically. This type of investing is rapidly becoming standard business practice, and we are beginning to see advertising and marketing cropping up everywhere as entrepreneurs begin to make their mark.

The history of buying at a lower price than "retail" began after World War II when Congress nullified the law requiring retailers to sell their goods at a price set by the manufacturer. After this happened, stores began to sell products at a lower price (think "on sale") to bring in customers and increase their market presence. Selling at prices lower than retail meant accepting a lower profit margin, but the stores found the increase in sales volume made up for the decreased profit margin, and then some.

The industry responded to this new concept of discounted merchandise by developing different types of financing and distribution programs. People began to fill roles such as manufacturing representatives, merchandise brokers, and wholesale buyers. By creating win-win situations for all parties, these people established very profitable businesses for themselves.

Wal-Mart's Sam Walton is a great example of someone who sold huge quantities of products to the masses by lowering the prices on the brand-name products people wanted to buy.

This book will focus on how to use the concepts of buying a product or service at below market value price, then turning it around for a profit. The areas of cash flow investing we will cover are:

- Real Estate Properties
- Real Estate Notes
- Factoring Invoices
- Other Debt Instruments

The guide will also give great examples and information on setting up a business; two chapters will be devoted to marketing your company and services. You will gain great insight into goal setting and learn how to improve yourself to create success and profitability in your life and your business.

All of the cash flow investing concepts will follow the same basic pattern. Let's go over the steps involved, so you can see how it applies to each area. Some areas will have fewer steps or will modify one or more steps, but the same basic process appears in all of them.

- Research
- Marketing
- Contact
- Information Gathering
- Paperwork
- Due Diligence
- Closing and Payment

You will see these steps repeated in each of these areas. It will give you a sense of how they apply in all areas.

Let's begin the book now, with a chapter that talks about how to set up your business from the beginning.

Chapter 1

Beginning with a Plan

In beginning your career, you need to make the commitment to give it your all. If you put in only a little effort, you will receive only a little return. Decide from the start to make your business work, and then put in the work and energy to make it happen. One of the first things you need to do is establish your company and image.

Type of Company

You will need to decide what type of company to form. Do you want a sole proprietorship, a partnership, or a corporation? Your goals will help you decide which of these to choose. An attorney or tax advisor can advise you on the tax advantages and legal protection that will be best for your situation.

Sole Proprietorship

A sole proprietorship is the least complicated and easiest to establish and maintain. A single person who makes all decisions and is responsible for all debts owns the business. This type of business offers the owner the most control. A sole proprietorship can make it easier to obtain loans, as banks will look at personal and company assets as collateral; however, this can be a huge disadvantage if you default on your loans. A sole proprietor risks unlimited personal liability.

For tax purposes, you and your businesses are one. At tax time, you report all of your business income and expenses on your personal tax return. When you use this method, you normally do not pay additional federal or state taxes on the business. You can also take advantage of tax-deferred retirement programs if you are a sole proprietor. Additionally, you can deduct business expenses such as meals, travel, and mileage.

The only paperwork you must file is a fictitious or assumed name statement if your company name is something other than your own name. This allows people who deal with your company to determine the owner's name.

General Partnership

A general partnership consists of two or more owners who share the profits and responsibilities. A partnership agreement defines the legal arrangement. There are two types of partnerships: general and limited. A general partnership means the partners contribute resources as well as share profits and responsibilities. The amount of contribution may or may not be equal, but each partner is equally responsible for debts. A general partnership can also utilize the varied skills of its partners to create areas of strengths.

The disadvantages of a general partnership are similar to those of a sole proprietorship with one notable exception. Each partner may face personal liability for the debts and actions of the business. The exception is that each partner does not have full control as in a sole proprietorship. Any action taken by any partner can affect the other partners and the business, even if he or she did not have the approval or consent of the other partners. This can create management conflicts and expose all the partners to potential risk.

Limited Partnership

A limited partnership is similar to a general partnership, except that one or more of the partners is "limited" and does not participate in the management or operation of the business. Limited partners are usually passive investors who only contribute money to the business. They also have limited liability in proportion to the size of their contribution.

People usually create limited partnerships to raise capital for a company. However, they can be expensive and complicated to establish. You must register limited partnerships and pay fees in most states. However, a limited partnership can be a win-win situation for both the limited partner/investor and the company receiving the infusion of capital.

Corporations

A corporation is a business entity owned by a group of stockholders. Stock represents ownership in the corporation. A group of people or an individual creates a corporation and then issues stock. A single person or a group of people may hold all of the stock. Corporations are the most difficult and expensive business structures to create and operate. But a corporation provides the most protection from personal liability.

A corporation exists as a separate entity from the owners. The corporation must file its own taxes, is responsible for its own debts, and conducts its own affairs. The individual owners are not liable for any actions of the corporation. The only risk the owners of a corporation face is losing the money they have invested in the company.

A corporation must have its own bank accounts and credit. Keep all business transactions separate from personal ones. Never use corporate funds interchangeably with personal funds, even if you are the sole employee of a corporation.

Establishing a corporation is time consuming and expensive. You must comply with federal, state, and local regulations. There are three types of corporations to consider.

C Corporation

A regular (or "C") corporation is a separate tax-paying entity. Any profit is subject to taxation. If the corporation distributes income to stockholders, the government taxes it again as income to stockholders. This double taxation can become a problem if the stockholders are also owners. Regular corporations can take advantage of certain tax advantages that can help offset this.

Subchapter S Corporation

A subchapter S corporation offers the same limited liability, but is not subject to corporate income tax. Owners of a subchapter S corporation pay income tax just like a sole proprietor. The corporation's profit appears on each stockholder's personal income tax return. This is an attractive type of corporation, but there are some restrictions.

Limited Liability Company

Like a regular corporation, this type of structure provides owners with limited liability, but you can allocate business profit differently than ownership interests for tax purposes. An LLC provides greater flexibility in some situations.

Company Name

Next, you need to decide on a company name. Determine if you want to use your own name or create a "company" name. You can have the company name be whatever you like, from a variation of your name such as Fred Harris and Associates, or something you make up like Trinity Investments. But be careful that the name you decide on creates an identity establishing who you are and what you do. You don't want potential clients wondering if they have reached the right person because your company name is too vague. Also, don't try to be "cute." You want your name to convey professionalism.

If you decide to use a fictitious name, contact your county or city courthouse to determine if someone else has already registered the name. Sometimes you can do this online if your city or county has a Web site. You may also want to obtain an Employer Identification Number by filing a form SS-4 with the IRS. If you are a sole proprietor, you can use your social security number instead.

You can use certain words that will help to give your company name a "presence." Words like American, Atlantic, international, nationwide, Pacific, and global all create a sense of stability with their geographic sound. Power words like creative, first, diversified, capital, and funding give the name a financial or powerful ring.

The end of your name is also important, so use words like associates, funding, network, source, services, group, ventures, corporation, or company to create a presence for your company.

Company Image

The next step is to decide how your clients will contact you. Will you use your home telephone line, a cell phone, or a dedicated business line? You want to project a professional image, so using your home number for business is probably not a good idea, especially if you have children who may answer the phone. You don't want potential clients or partners to decide they don't want to do business with you because they feel you are not professional. Remember that old adage, "You never get a second chance to make a first impression."

Another thing that reflects on your professionalism is your business card. Your business card will help you establish yourself as a professional and develop that image for others. It is also an important marketing tool because you can give your card to everyone you meet. Even if people you give your card to are not in the market for your services, they may encounter someone who IS. In this way, you can network your business simply by giving out your card. Make sure you have quality cards designed and printed. You want your cards to look professional and convey that image to others.

At the same time, you can design and print stationary and envelopes. Like your business cards, a business letterhead and envelope will convey professionalism to your clients and partners. Come up with a logo that relates to your field. You can either design your own or hire a professional. Place your logo on your letterhead, envelopes, and business cards. You want your business image to be unified and recognizable.

You may also want a short tag line associated with your company image, something that "tells what you do." This can be simple or a slogan of sorts. Additionally, you will want to come up with a title. Stay away from the title of broker, however, because it can be misleading.

We have placed several pages of blank "business cards" in the appendix for you to sketch out possible designs. Make sure you put the following on your business card.

- Business Name
- Tag Line
- Your Name
- Address
- Telephone Number
- Fax Number
- E-mail address and/or Web site URL

You may be interested in obtaining a post office box instead of using your home address. This is especially true if you live on a street with a whimsical or homey-sounding name, such as Babbling Brook Court. A post office box will provide your company with a separate address for your mail, and will keep your home address more secure. You can also utilize a mail service, which will have an actual street address and "suite" number. This can lend more credence to your company than a PO box number.

Office Supplies and Other Details

You will want to set up your office, whether in an office building or at home. Organize your supplies for maximum efficiency. You want to be able to easily locate forms you need when talking to potential clients on the phone.

Purchase the necessary office equipment—fax machine, computer, filing cabinets, business calculators, etc. Buy office supplies such as pens, computer paper, file folders, and whatever else you need to stay organized. Stacking trays are great for keeping different forms handy, but separate.

Open a separate business account at your bank. You need to ensure that you keep your business and personal expenses separate. Keep an expanding folder for business receipts. Buy a mileage booklet and track all business-related mileage.

Once you have the details of setting up your business, you can move on to marketing your services. The next two chapters deal with the subject of traditional marketing and Internet marketing.

Chapter 2

Marketing Strategies

In order to begin making money, you must first find clients. Your marketing plan is the way to create a client base. The marketing efforts of your business can determine the success or failure of your company, so take them seriously. You must do initial marketing in order to gain a client base, but you will quickly run out of clients if you do not continue your efforts. It must be a continuing process, always bringing in more clients for you.

Although you may be focusing on only one area of cash flow investing, such as factoring or real estate, this chapter will give good information that you can tailor to fit your market segment. Obviously, if you are going to focus on real estate, you should narrow your marketing efforts to those people who are buying or selling homes. The same goes for the other areas we will discuss.

First, let's talk about two different kinds of advertising—general and targeted. In general advertising, you are putting your name and advertisement "out there" for the masses. Many people might see your advertisement, but they may not be the people who would become your clients.

Targeted marketing narrows your advertising and marketing efforts to a smaller group of people or companies—ones that would most likely need your services—and focus your efforts on them. It may take more time to develop a targeted list of contacts and may cost more money than general advertising, but because it focuses on the group of people who are most likely to be receptive to your message, it can be the best way to gain clients. Telephone marketing, personal visits, direct mail and e-mails are all great ways to target your marketing efforts.

Using some of both types of advertising/marketing is the best way to get your message to the public. The best way to plan your marketing efforts is to take it a step at a time. Let's look at the steps:

- Research — develop lists of people to contact
- Materials — develop the materials you will send, such as brochures, mailers, etc.
- Implement and Evaluate — go forward with your marketing efforts and determine how effective each type of advertisement is working

Research

You cannot target your marketing materials to a group of contacts until you have developed a list. Research is very important so you don't waste your time sending letters and brochures to people who are just going to throw them away. You want to target people who will receive it. They are the ones who will most likely read it and want more information.

The way to begin is to think about what your potential clients want and need. Ask yourself what you would want from a service provider if you were in their situation. Create a client profile of the people and businesses that would benefit from what you offer. For example, if you were a factoring broker, then your initial list would include small to medium-sized companies.

You will also want to develop a list of direct contact sources. These people encounter your potential clients. Examples would include attorneys, accountants, and bankers. These people can give you valuable referrals of people they work with on a daily basis.

One way to group or target your potential candidates is to determine whom your funding sources will accept. If you are working in the factoring arena, then the factors you work with may have certain criteria you must meet. If you are working in real estate notes, then the investors may have requirements as to the amount or terms of the notes. You need to be able to break down your list to meet the requirements of the funding sources you are working with.

Once you have determined the specifics, begin to compile your list with the candidates that fit the requirements of the market segment you want to target. Gather as much information on each candidate as possible, with a minimum being name, address, and telephone number.

You may have to research public records, obtain mailing lists for clubs and organizations geared toward your segment, or use a list broker to find people who meet your criteria. Develop your list of direct contact sources at the same time. Use the yellow pages to find people in your area who will work with you. Call them or send a letter introducing your services and asking for referrals. This small effort can produce a stream of clients for you.

Materials

The next step is to decide what types of marketing materials you would like to utilize, and then design and print them. In your research-gathering efforts, you may get an idea of the best way to market to your particular target group. A free seminar may be a way to get your message across to business professionals. Direct mail or postcards may be a good way to target homeowners. Telephone marketing is great method of ensuring that your message makes it to the decision maker rather than the trash.

Your marketing materials are critical in establishing your company image. It may be the first impression you make on potential clients. This impression depends on how well you communicate who you are, what you do, and how they can benefit from your service.

Your materials must have a clear focus and must address their needs, showing them how you can solve their problems. People will become your clients if you can show them what's in it for them. If you want them to respond, show them how you can make their lives better. You have only a few seconds to make your impression, so you need to grab their attention from the start.

Using client testimonials is a good way to get people to pay attention to your message. If they can see that you provide results and others are happy with your service, they are more likely to take a chance on you. Once you have developed a client base, ask your existing clients what problems you solved for them and how they felt about working with your company. These testimonials can motivate prospects to call you.

Above all, be honest and concise. People don't want to be conned, and most people are skeptical about any new product and service. Don't make exaggerated claims. Lies and deception will only hurt your credibility and professional image in the long run.

You also want to stay away from talking about things that do not motivate the person to action. Things like how long you have been in business, the people who work for your company, and where you are located may be pertinent information after people have become clients, but they don't care about those things when they are deciding whether to trash your letter. Focus on them and their problems. Show them how you and your services can make their problems go away. Show them the value of what you can do for them.

So what are some different types of marketing materials you should develop?

Direct Mail

The first method is to develop a direct mail campaign. In a direct mail campaign, you can utilize letters or postcards to get your message to the public, but there are a couple of things to remember.

First, you want to make sure your marketing literature is getting to the correct decision maker. If you address your letter "To Whom It May Concern," it will probably end up in the trash at the receptionist's desk. Once you have a name, you can customize your postcards or letters to go directly to the person who will best understand what you are trying to offer, and be able to make a decision.

The other thing to remember is that you want to catch readers' attention right off the bat. Most recipients of unsolicited mail open it and scan it quickly before they throw it out. If your postcard or letter grabs people's attention, then you have guaranteed they will read on.

Use an attention-grabbing headline such as "INCREASE YOUR CASH FLOW TODAY" if your area of expertise is factoring. Put this at the top of the letter or postcard, even before a name and address. You want your readers to continue. Your first paragraph should then expand on your headline and keep readers' attention.

You want your prospects to read this first paragraph and ask, "How?" Keep your first paragraph friendly and simple. You want to think about the questions your reader will have when he or she is finished reading so you can answer them in the following paragraphs. Then continue your letter to inform potential customers of how you can SOLVE THEIR PROBLEMS! They don't care what you do! You need to hook them with the way you can make their lives easier. Later in the process, you can explain all the benefits of working with you. Right up front, you want them to see how their problems can go away.

Include a "tear off" reply section at the bottom of the letter or a reply card they can mail back to you for more information. This reply section/card should say something like, "Yes, please tell me more_____," and then include lines for them to write all their contact information such as name, address, company, e-mail, phone numbers, etc.

Another letter you can use to market your services can explain more of your services right in the body of the letter. Make sure the top of the letter still contains a headline that will attract readers' attention. After all, you want them to read the rest.

In the body of the letter, make sure the information presented gives readers a chance to identify with the circumstances discussed. You want them to say, "Gee, I'm in the same boat." Discuss how you can solve their problems, how your services will work, and give them an invitation to call if they want to discuss it further.

Appendix B contains sample letters and forms you can change to fit your particular prospecting circumstances.

If you create a "tickler" file that contains the details of each of your mailings, you can easily keep track of multiple mailings to the same contact list. By sending three or four letters, you can keep your name in front of contacts until they are ready to become clients.

Flyers and Postcards

Another marketing device is a flyer. You can send flyers with your marketing letters or use them alone. They are inexpensive to make, but they get attention and can send business your way. The key to developing a good flyer is to get your message across as simply as possible. It's not a letter so feel free to use bullets, large type, or anything that can convey your message in the space provided. Explain how your services will solve problems; don't just say what you do. For example,

XYZ Factoring buys your business invoices for cash!
VS.
Get cash today for those invoices that aren't due for three months!

The first example tells people what you do. This is admirable since you will most likely get some business this way; however, the second example shows companies how to solve the problem of getting cash flow now. You can design these types of headlines for any cash flow investing area you are pursuing.

Postcards are another way to get your marketing efforts into the hands of those who can benefit from them. Postcards should be well designed because they are like mini flyers, showing how your potential clients can solve their problems by working with you. Postcards are cheaper to mail than letters, and can achieve the same results By altering the colors and fonts of your postcard message, you can send the same basic postcard to the same list of contacts several times to keep your name in front of them.

Brochures

Probably the most important part of your marketing literature should be a brochure. A brochure will provide details that can't be included in a flyer. In a brochure, you can explain your services in detail, as well as why a potential client should work with you rather then someone else. Make sure the brochure is well planned, attractive, and conveys a professional image for your business.

Fax Marketing

Faxing your marketing letter is a great way to get your message out for much less than postage. Develop a one-page information sheet that lists your company name, the services you offer, and how prospects can reach you. By faxing this to potential clients and direct contact sources, you are able to save time and money.

You can send your faxes at night when long distance rates are generally cheaper. Most companies leave their fax machines on overnight. Some companies send out faxes this way for a minimal charge.

Please note that you cannot send unsolicited faxes. You must call and obtain permission first. It is illegal to send unsolicited faxes.

Web Pages and E-mail

In the next chapter, we will discuss Internet Marketing in much more detail. However, let's take a brief look at your marketing options here.

A very effective method of advertising on the Internet is to develop a Web page that can inform the public about your business and create deals for you. Web pages can be set up to contain forms to collect information from clients and potential clients, saving you steps down the road.

Design your Web page so you can educate potential clients about your services, while at the same time motivating them to find out more by contacting you. The beauty of a Web page is that you are not limited by space. You can put as much or as little information on it as you like. By using links and menus, you can direct your visitors to different areas where they can learn more about your business. "Autoresponders" can be set up to send more information automatically when people request it through your Web site.

Another important thing to remember in designing a Web site is that it needs to be easy to navigate. Make sure people can easily find your company name and logo at the top of the home page. Design each separate page to have a unified background and "look," so that your visitors get a sense of the site as a whole, no matter what page they are on. Use bullets and other organizational aids when presenting information so your page is easy to scan for information. Most people will not read every word.

You can use feedback forms to allow your visitors to reach you, request information, or give you contact information.

E-mail is another way to "direct mail" contact lists. The next chapter describes e-mail marketing in detail and shows how you can utilize this powerful tool.

Implement and Evaluate

There are other ways to advertise your services. Below is a list of different methods. Take a look and see which ones will work for you.

- Print Advertising (newspapers, magazines, trade journals)
- Trade Shows
- Networking
- Public Speaking
- TV and Radio
- Gifts and Novelties•
- Billboards and Bulletin Boards
- Referrals

Print Advertising

Develop a basic ad briefly explaining who you are and what you do. Make it informative, and always include the various ways clients can contact you (phone, e-mail, mailing address). Offer free information or a no-obligation consultation to spur readers' to action.

Place the ad where it will get the most attention from the people you are trying to attract. You can utilize the business and real estate sections of your local newspaper or advertise in magazines that cater to your target audience. You can also take advantage of local community papers and "ad papers" like the *Penny Saver* or *Thrifty Nickel*. Because advertising space is cheap in these local papers, you can afford to place a larger ad than you could in a large regional paper.

Other areas to think about are:

- Business Organization Newsletters
- Professional Newsletters
- Newsletters of Direct Contact Sources
- National Trade Journals
- Professional Magazines

In addition to simply placing an ad, you can create exposure for your company by using press releases, articles, interviews, and business announcements. Use press releases to provide information to a newspaper or magazine. When you start your business, you should issue a press release to announce your presence in the marketplace. Then, from time to time, issue other press releases when important things happen.

Press releases should have a simple, direct style that states the five W's—who, what, where, when, and why. Do not make it sound like an advertisement; it should convey information. You will want to have a headline that catches an editor's eye to increase your chances for publication. See Appendix B for sample press releases.

Submitting articles to business and trade journals is an excellent way to expose your business to a group of potential clients. There are four parts to a good article: the lead, the nut graph, the body, and the conclusion.

The lead should open the article and explain the problem or situation. Design it to capture and hold the reader's interest. The nut graph expands on the information presented in the lead and sets the tone for the rest of the article. The body should develop the nut graph using quotes, information, and statistics. These three parts should flow smoothly and convey a unified message. The conclusion should relate back to the lead by concluding the opening statement, answering the questions raised, or summarizing the article.

If you make the article a sales piece, editors will reject it. A true article is designed to inform and bring interest; it does not sell your services. If you want to do that, you can write what is known as an "advertorail," which is an article that is usually a paid advertisement. In this piece, you can promote yourself and your services as much as you like because you are paying for the advertising space.

Interviews are another way to get your message out to the public, but they have an important side function. When people hear or see your interview, they see you as an authority figure. It increases your creditability in your field. Contact the editors of your local newspapers and trade journals. Offer to be interviewed for upcoming articles that deal with your field of cash flow investing.

Many newspapers and business journals also have a separate section for business announcements. A business announcement is short and to the point, reporting on the activities of a company. The announcement can be about new services or interesting information about the company. For information on submission, contact the business editor of the publication in which you would like to place your announcement.

Trade Shows

Trade shows are a good place to find potential clients and direct contact sources. They typically have a theme that determines the group of people that will be interested in attending. Trade shows can be national, regional, or local. You can market yourself at a trade show by:

- Becoming an exhibitor and maintain a booth at the show
- Networking with exhibitors at the show
- Networking with attendees of the show

Always bring plenty of business cards and brochures when you are going to a trade show, so you can give information and a card to everyone you talk to. You can contact your local convention or visitors bureau for a list of upcoming trade shows in your area.

Networking

When we talked about business cards, we mentioned how important it is to hand your card to everyone you meet. Networking is a vital part of your marketing efforts, because you never know when someone will give your card to a friend or acquaintance who may need your help.

Focus especially on professionals who have regular contact with your target client base (direct contact sources). You want to develop relationships with their people so they are willing to refer their clients to you. You may want to pay a referral fee, or at least send a thank you note for each deal they send your way.

Remember that your professionalism will reflect back on them, so treat your clients with respect and courtesy. The last thing you want to happen is for one of your referrals to return to the person who referred him or her and express dissatisfaction with you. That will be the last referral you get from that source.

Try to refer business back to them as well. It will create a win-win situation for both of you. Networking works both ways. As you get clients and meet other direct contact sources, refer business to them as well. You will find that more and more people will be "working" to send business to you.

Public Speaking

Another opportunity to expand your reach is to volunteer to speak for community group meetings. The newspaper will tell you where and when these groups meet. Call the contact people and offer your time. Give them a brief description of what you will talk about, but don't try to sell them. They only want to book speakers. Groups like Kiwanis, Lions, and Rotary clubs all meet regularly. You can also contact your local chamber of commerce for more information.

Before you speak, create a simple twenty-minute presentation about your services. Include information about the industry to educate them instead of merely selling yourself. Hand out educational written materials at your speeches. These materials will also have your name and number on them, but offer your listeners more than just a business card. Practice in front of others so you can get used to speaking with an audience.

TV and Radio

Like the public speaking engagements, you can also volunteer to talk on a radio or television program. Local cable channels have opportunities for guest appearances. Local TV talk shows are interested in professionals like you. Radio programs can be a good way to go as well. Even network television can have a place for you. If you find programs that would appeal to your target audience, contact the producer of the show and offer to be a guest.

As before, put together a concept that will work with a show's format, and make sure it relates to your area of business. Present the concept to the producer. If interested, he or she may arrange a meeting, and then schedule you to appear on the show.

You can present your concepts to local television and radio stations as well. Make yourself available on short notice so that if someone else cancels, the station has you as a backup. Give your phone number often and leave a data sheet with the station secretary so callers can get more information on how to contact you.

Gifts and Novelties

You can promote your business and help people remember you by giving away gifts and novelties. These are generally inexpensive items with your logo, name, and phone number. These types of things are usually pens, mugs, key chains, calendars, etc.

You can use these "giveaways" to show appreciation for referrals, as a thank you to direct contact sources, and to help your clients keep your name in front of them. People always like to get free things, so it can greatly help your public relations. However, the greatest benefit is the fact that even if people throw away your business card or letter, they may hold on to your pen or mouse pad—and that means they always have your name and number within reach.

Billboards and Bulletin Boards

For general advertising, billboards and bulletin boards can reach a huge audience for a minimal cost. The best way to find a billboard to use is to look for those that are currently empty. The owner of the billboard is losing money every day no one is renting the space, so you may be able to negotiate a better deal. Billboards offer great exposure.

Another great way to get your name and service to the public is to utilize community bulletin boards. Community bulletin boards are everywhere from libraries to grocery stores. Place a flyer on several of these boards and see which ones gain you the most leads. You want the flyers you place on bulletin boards to draw eyes and attention, so make them catchy and a quick read. Put the time and effort into developing a great flyer so it catches people's attention and keeps it.

Referrals

Direct contact sources are a good way to gain business through referrals. These professionals encounter people who could be your clients. Depending on the type of cash flow investing you are doing, the list of direct contact sources will change. Each of the chapters in this book has its own list of the types of people who work out well as direct contact sources for that particular field.

Remember to give them your card and information so they know how to contact you. Send referrals to them so they will be willing to reciprocate. Even if you can't develop a personal relationship with each one, at least try to get on a referral list they give their clients. Referrals are a great way to build your business.

Once you have developed and implemented a marketing plan, you must periodically take the time to evaluate how your efforts are working for your business. Determine what is working and what is not. Are you spending marketing dollars for an ad in the newspaper that never draws any business? Are most of your clients coming from direct contact sources or somewhere else?

By asking clients how they heard of you, you can quickly pinpoint which of your marketing efforts are worth spending more money on and which are not. Once you find out what is bringing in clients, boost your efforts in that area.

You can also evaluate your materials by seeing which ads or other materials bring in the most clients. Always make sure it is easy for your customers to figure out how to reach you and that your material prompts them to action. When other advertisements and direct mail comes across your desk, take a look at it and determine if it interests you or prompts you to action. It will help you to see examples of effective advertising, and help you to see what not to do. You can do the same with advertising in other media as well. Make sure your evaluation is an ongoing process so you can quickly fix things that need improving.

Chapter 3

Internet Marketing Ideas

Advertising in a traditional magazine can cost $30,000 or more for a full-page ad! You have to get the ad to the magazine in advance, and you won't start to see leads until the month after publication. That is a lot of money up front and a long time to wait to see results.

Online, you can run the ad, see how the public responds and start taking orders immediately, which translates into money in your pocket. You can test as many variations of the advertisement as you like to determine which one is the most successful.

That's what makes advertising on the Internet one of the most cost-effective marketing solutions you can use. This chapter will discuss different ways to use e-mail and the Internet to reach your target audience.

E-mail

E-mail has become one of the most utilized forms of communication in use today! Why? Because it's free, it's instant, and it's everywhere. Think about it. Aren't you stunned when someone says he or she doesn't have e-mail? So to begin with, let's talk about some tools to use to send your e-mails out.

Easy Tools to Use

1. Eudora (www.eudora.com): This is an e-mail client that takes the time-consuming task of daily e-mail management and makes it very easy. You can choose one of three versions:
  - Sponsored Version —provides you with the full-featured version of Eudora for free and there are static on-screen ads that don't interfere with your e-mail workspace

- Paid Version —provides you with a full-featured version without the ads
- Lite Version —provides a free, reduced feature version with no ads

There really is no difference in the sponsored and paid versions, except the ads, and they are easily ignored. It is important to save your e-mail into different mailboxes for later reference. It's simple with Eudora. This helps keep your e-mail organized so you don't accidentally miss an important message when you may be getting hundreds of e-mails per week. You can also use many different mailboxes. You should use your in-box for messages you need to answer immediately. Then they can go to the appropriate mailbox.

Channels (www.pacificwebworks.com): This program is simple to use. It builds and maintains your lists so you can use them online, and continually backs them up. You can download the files to use as a database if you desire, and you can easily personalize all of your e-mails for follow-up sales.

- Allows you to personalize your mailings, by merging up to one hundred fields into your e-mail messages (things like first and last names and other pertinent information). This small benefit makes people assume you really know them. Your message is professional and is less likely to be deleted before it is read.

- Automatically places each person's own e-mail address in the "To" field. They realize you sent it directly to them and it is not spam. There is less chance of getting filtered out.

- Filters out duplicate addresses and duplicate domain names. You really will look like a spammer if someone gets duplicate e-mails. This is an easy way to edit your customer database.

- Starts and stops mailings at any point and picks up exactly where you left off. What would happen if you lost your Internet connection in the middle of your mailing? You wouldn't know who had been mailed to already, and you would have to start over at the beginning.

- Cleans out your e-mail database and removes undeliverables.

- Automatically subscribes and unsubscribes people to your newsletter.

- Automatically replies to incoming mail with the right message.

- Captures and stores contact information in your custom database.

- Extracts e-mail addresses from any file on your computer and organizes them into a simple database.

- Automates repetitive chores, saving you a substantial amount of time.

- Runs multiple newsletters from anywhere—you don't have to be at your own computer.

- Gives your leads a second chance to try your services by sending them an e-mail. The more times they hear from you, the more leads you convert into customers.

- The program can be set to send both text and HTML formats at the same time, and automatically detects which format each subscriber's e-mail browser can read.

So now that you have some ideas of which program to use for your e-mailing, how do you begin to use e-mail to really bring in business? There are three ways to go about marketing your business.

- E-mail your customers directly with your sales letter.

- E-mail your customers directly with information that will

be of interest, and then direct them to your sales letter via hyperlink.

- E-mail other online businesses that deal with your target customers and arrange for them to promote or sell your product on their sites.

No matter what method you choose, there are key steps you should follow to ensure success rather than dismal failure.

Target your customers: Make sure the list you use for your e-mail campaign is not a random list of "everyone." You want to make sure you are targeting the people who will be interested in your services. It is a waste of your money to buy lists with a million people on them if they couldn't care less about your service. The people you should be targeting are those who have opted in to your mailing list, customers and leads, and people that have requested information from your marketing effort.

Personalize your e-mails: People are more likely to read your e-mail if it is addressed personally to them, and doesn't look like Spam! Consider checking out our software options that will allow you to customize your e-mails using a database of customer information.

Have a good subject line: Good subject lines, like good headlines, can make all the difference between an e-mail that someone reads and one that gets deleted. The key is to emphasize benefits. Think about how your services benefit your customers. You can probably take notes from your sales letter. How will they benefit or learn from reading this e-mail? Will it save them money or improve their lives? Your subject line should emphasize these benefits.

The first paragraph must count: Summarize your entire sales pitch in the first paragraph. It may be all your potential clients read. Continue to build the excitement of your subject line by explaining how your service will solve their problems. Make them curious enough to read on.

Test it first: It is very important to test your e-mail on a small sample of the list before sending it out to everyone. You can test your marketing e-mail and see what kind of response you get. It really comes down to this—do you want to waste your whole list on an e-mail that gets a so-so response, only to find out that your second draft increased your response by 400%? By sending out "trial run" e-mails, you can test all parts of your marketing campaign cheaply and easily, saving you time and money in the long run.

Easy reading: Make sure your e-mail is easy to read or people will click the delete key. Keep your e-mails simple and neat with lots of white space. Don't use technical terms that will confuse your potential customers. Don't use all caps since it is hard to read and considered as "yelling" in the world of e-mail and chat. Avoid text art and graphics, as some older e-mail programs may not support them.

Easy to reply: Make sure the e-mail addresses and URLs listed in your e-mail are easy for the customer to click directly on. Most e-mail programs will automatically pull up a new mail message or a new browser window if your links are set up correctly. E-mail hyperlinks should include the "mailto:" prefix. This will allow the e-mail program to launch a new e-mail, making it easy for the customer to reply. URLs should include the "http://" so the program will launch the browser and go directly to the site mentioned. You should also try to keep all of your Web addresses in lower case to avoid confusion with upper versus lower case. And be careful not to put a period after a URL. You don't want the computer thinking the period is part of the Web address.

"Sign" your e-mails: Develop an electronic signature to attach to the bottom of all your e-mails. It is also called a "sig file." Include your name, your e-mail address, your telephone number, company name, etc. This is free advertising if you use it correctly. Use it to "sign" your name to any posting you make in mailing lists or forums. It is legitimate information that you now have available to anyone who reads your posts. Use a variety of sig files to target different customers, newsgroups, lists, etc. It makes for very effective advertising.

How to Collect Targeted E-mail Addresses

First of all, don't just collect e-mail addresses. It's a waste of effort, and you could be accused of spamming. Secondly, you get a much better response from a targeted list of previous clients, newsletter subscribers, and visitors who have opted in to your e-mail database.

You can gather them from your Web site guest book, free offers, autoresponder logs (people who have requested information from you in the past), and anyone who has asked for more information. These people will not accuse you of spamming, because they have given you their e-mail addresses.

Collecting addresses from other groups and chat areas is a bad idea; they are usually protective of their privacy and don't want ads clogging their e-mail. They have not given you permission to use their addresses and WILL accuse you of spamming. Spamming is now illegal in most states and if convicted, you could face huge fines as well as jail time.

There are many places and Web sites from which to obtain addresses, but many people now use software that automatically deletes e-mail from unknown users. So it is best to use e-mail addresses of people who have already dealt with you.

Hyperlink Techniques

In real estate, the cliché is "location, location, location." Giants in business have their names everywhere. Online should be no different. Amazon.com is a perfect example. Their business is at every major Web "intersection."

Well-thought-out linking techniques attract large amounts of targeted traffic. If you put your site on a major Web "intersection," you will ensure your site receives a steady flow of potential clients. When people access a Web site they like and find a link to your site, they believe your business to be credible too. They click to your Web page and are open to your offers, because your credibility was established back at the other page, long before they got to yours. Here are a few more pointers:

You must research your linking prospects: Web sites that deal directly with YOUR target market should have some good information you can use. The Web sites should contain their home page (URL), address, name of owner, e-mail address, and a brief description of what the site is about. Collect detailed information you can use to request a link with them. The more information you include the more personal it will be and more likely they will take it seriously.

Use a table or database to organize your list: You need to stay organized so you know from whom you've requested a link, who has requested one from you, and whom you need to contact again. Set up a database or spreadsheet right from the start to keep your information clear and concise.

Divide your prospects into two lists and rate them. The primary list should include those sites you most want a link from. You want them complementary, not competitive to yours. This is when you want to collect those extra bits of personalized information to use in contacting them. The secondary list is for sites that are related to your target market, but are not as focused or might not have enough traffic.

Write a personalized e-mail to those on your primary list. Comment on their Web sites, describe who you are, and say why you are e-mailing them. Emphasize the "win-win" potential of your relationship. Give details about how easy is to link, and be sure to give them your contact information. Make it as personalized as possible. Make a template of this letter where you can quickly fill in the blanks. Here's an example of an e-mail you might use to request a link...

Hi (first name),

I visited your Web site at (insert URL here) and noticed your resources page has (insert personal comments here).

I want to mention we have a Web site that educates customers on (insert description) by providing them with quality information at (http://www.yoursite.com).

This would obviously fit perfectly into your resource page, and I am sure your visitors would appreciate your providing them with such valuable information that will save time and money. They'll view your Web site even more favorably and be likely to return again and again.

It's clearly a win-win situation for both of us. Linking to my site is extremely easy. All you have to do is (enter process to link).

The best part about this is that the links could funnel traffic to your Web site for years to come. So take plenty of time to work on building mutually beneficial relationships with them.

Write a personalized e-mail to those on your secondary list. You don't need to spend much time on their Web sites, but become familiar with them so you can personalize each letter. You have to organize your table or database so that you CAN personalize and keep track of what you do.

Be persistent and keep trying. If they don't respond to your first e-mail, up the ante. Offer to exchange links. If you are a cooperative business, not a competitive one, it might work. Give them the exact HTML code to put on their Web page. Don't just say, "Let's exchange links." The easier it is for them to link to you, the higher the probability they will. If they have to go through several e-mails to get the specifics out of you, they may not do it. Be sure you have a contact telephone number in your message, and the hours they can call you. Talking directly to people helps to build the rapport and credibility necessary to get the link. This technique is extremely valuable. It will bring you more visitors every month. Just look at how effective it is when you surf the Net; you almost always click on a link and go somewhere else.

Viral Marketing

You know how a flu virus can spread from one person to many others? Viral marketing follows the same concept. It allows you to exponentially increase your visibility online by turning your existing network of clients and direct contact sources into a giant word-of-mouth referral machine.

Hotmail is a very good example of viral marketing. Very simply, they add a small Hotmail advertisement to the bottom of every e-mail sent by a user of the Hotmail system. The person receiving an e-mail from the user of Hotmail thinks this must be a good idea, because his or her friend has an account with them. So he signs up too by clicking on the link.

Hotmail has developed the ultimate referral system. Users advertise and promote it every time they send an e-mail. In twelve months, Hotmail built a multimillion-dollar business using this one simple viral marketing technique.

Viral marketing is a very good technique to copy. It exponentially increases the visibility of your business. People like to tell about their experiences, especially online, even more so than a good restaurant. With good quality service, clients are more than willing to tell others. And the power of these referrals lies in the snowball effect they can have on your business.

Credibility and trust are built when people spread the message about your service and reputation. They are giving you a personal recommendation, and this is powerful. People are very open to these third-party recommendations, because someone they know has already tried it. People who learn about your business from a friend or a relative already trust you.

Amazon.com uses this technique all the time. Every time people buy something, the company encourages them to send a gift to a friend or family member. With every gift people send, Amazon.com includes a flyer that promotes its products. It's a very subtle, but effective endorsement for Amazon.com.

Viral marketing actually compels people to DO something about your marketing message rather then just listen to it or watch it. This helps one to absorb it, remember it, and repeat it. Kind of like telling a joke you've heard. You'll remember it better if you repeat it soon after hearing it. One of your goals is to keep advertising costs low, and viral marketing does this well. Your clients and direct contact sources help do the advertising for you. By just adding a line such as, "Do you know someone who would be interested in reading this article? Click here to e-mail it to them," you can increase your market visibility as well as develop new leads. Remember to give the visitor some benefit for sharing, and TELL them to share.

Banner Marketing

A banner is simply a graphic that businesses use to advertise their Web sites, basically like a billboard. It puts your advertising directly in front of your target market. When Internet surfers see your banner ad, they consider visiting a site they might not have otherwise looked at. It encourages people to action by "clicking here" to be taken directly to your Web site. A really good banner has certain criteria that are important to remember.

Clearly define your purpose: Decide what action you want people to take. Do you just want to increase exposure? Directly increase clients? Just click on your banner? Sign up for a free newsletter?

Focus on a benefit: Write your ad with your target customers in mind. Keep your message brief and use keywords. Build excitement, make them curious, but don't tell them you're selling something.

Call to action: Always tell people to "click here" or "go"—it's a call for action. Many people don't know that just clicking on a banner is a link to a Web site.

Here are a few other pointers to keep in mind when creating your online banner.

- Vibrant colors draw a better response than drab ones, but don't overdo it.

- Use mock "window control" buttons like menus and click boxes. Most people are familiar with these so their use subtly calls them to action.

- Make your banner fast loading. Size isn't everything, but it must be eye-catching.

- Automate your banner; it has a large advantage over static banners, because they catch people's attention with movement.

- Include an alternative text tag. This way, people who have their graphics turned off when surfing the Web will still see your slogan and your link.

- Your banner should be at the top of a page. It will get a much better response than at the bottom.

Test and track your results. Design several and test them to see which ones bring in the most traffic. If you don't make money with them, redesign them, or negotiate a better price for the ad space. Maybe you need to rewrite your sales copy to convince visitors to become clients. Your slogan may need to be better. By testing, you will know what works and what doesn't.

Now that we have finished our discussion of marketing, let's move on to our chapters that give details about the different areas of cash flow investing. The next few chapters that discuss the specific areas of cash flow investing will be structured differently than the rest of the book. These chapters will present information more in a reference style with fewer formal paragraphs and information that is more detailed.

Chapter 4

Real Estate Investment

The real estate market is a cash flow business that revolves around buying, selling, trading, financing, leasing, and restructuring all types of properties. It's a business that anyone with the proper knowledge can get into. You do not have to have a lot of money to begin investing in real estate, and you can own your own business wherever you live. You can decide what you want to do with the properties in which you invest, whether it is to buy and sell, or to hold them and rent them to others.

In America today, people are finding it harder and harder to own their own homes due to their inability to qualify for loans. Lending institutions are making their qualifying requirements tougher, and many people can't get traditional loans. Because of this, many people are willing to work out creative solutions in order to get into homes of their own.

You can enter the world of real estate investing to take advantage of this precise situation. Doing this takes surprisingly little of your own capital—in fact, you can do it with as few as three credit cards and some smart money handling.

In order to make money in real estate investing, you must find people who, for one reason or another, need to get out of their homes and are willing to do it at whatever cost they can. Perhaps someone is building a new home that is almost complete, and he or she doesn't want two mortgage payments. Or maybe a person has been transferred elsewhere for a job. It may be something unfortunate, such as divorce, illness, or a lost job. Whatever the reason, these people are motivated, even desperate, to sell their homes, even if it means they will lose some money.

With today's business climate, people change jobs, get downsized, transferred, or simply quit all the time. The average family moves once every five years. Long gone are the days when a family pays off a thirty-year mortgage by living in the house for thirty years! Because people are moving more often, it opens the door for you to buy and sell real estate—and make a terrific profit doing it!

All you have to do is find these motivated sellers, buy the property at a below-market-value price, and then create a situation where you can either sell or rent the property to bring in a profit.

Why to Invest in Real Estate

There are several reasons why investing in real estate is a worthy business venture for you. Several factors that affect this type of investment can bring you excellent returns on your money. These factors are: appreciation, equity, cash flow, and taxes.

Appreciation

Appreciation occurs when the value of a property increases over time. For example, if I buy a home in 2000 for $100,000, and I sell it in 2006 for $150,0000, I have realized $50,000 of appreciation. I did nothing to my home other than live in it for six years. That is the beauty of real estate—appreciation and time do a lot of the work for you. Many things can contribute to the appreciation of property—location, renovations or remodeling, additions, etc. Many older homes that used to be in remote locations, find themselves in the middle of new housing developments as cities spread outward. All these factors can increase the appreciation of a home's value.

Equity

Equity is similar to appreciation in that it is based on value. However, where appreciation is the difference in the original buying price and the current worth of the home, equity is the difference between what is owed on the property and its current worth. Using the example from above—I have been paying my monthly mortgage payment on my home for six years and, when I sell it, the remaining mortgage balance is $90,000. When I sell my house for $150,000, I have netted $60,000 in equity.

Cash Flow

Cash flow is the difference between money coming in versus money going out. For example, if you have rental or lease income of $1,000 on a property and the expenses for that same property are $800, you have a positive cash flow of $200 per month. The concept of cash flow applies mostly to rental properties where money is truly "flowing" in and out; however, if you are investing in real estate for sale and can move it quickly, cash flow can also be applied to the money received from the sales transaction.

Taxes

Tax write-offs and deductions can play a big factor in the amount of profit you receive in your business. Expenses, mileage, advertising, entertainment, meals, and your office expenditures can all create positive tax advantages for you when tax time rolls around. You can also write off the costs associated with fixing up properties. Any tax deduction that you would normally take on your taxes for your own residence can also be used for your investment properties, reducing your overall tax bill.

When investing in real estate, a wise entrepreneur finds a good deal and is then able to deliver it to an investor who wants it. This is how you make a profit. You must be able to find the right property to purchase, and then be able to hold it until you make a profit. If you aren't able to hold a property till the time is right, then you are in the same boat with the desperate seller who sold you the property!

Your best bet, however, is not to hold the property at all. Make sure that before you buy a property, you already know what you are going to do with it. Have a buyer already lined up before you buy. Know if you are going to rent it, lease it, sell it, trade it, etc. Have all of your plans outlined before you make the purchase.

Whatever you do when buying properties, you must keep emotions from influencing your business decisions. Because you are dealing with people, many times people who have fallen on hard times, it is difficult to keep emotions out of the equation. The decision to buy should be based on money—a simple monetary transaction.

You also must know and understand the area where you are working and investing. If you live in Southern California and are used to fixer-uppers going for $500,000 in some areas, and you then move to Oregon, you will have a skewed sense of the "right" price for a home. What would sell for a million dollars in Orange County may be a $250,000 home in Utah. Take the time to get to "know" the market where you are working so you can see what the going price is for all types of homes and properties. By doing this, you will be able to "estimate" the great deals and can move quickly to capitalize on them.

If you have trouble with "loving or hating" a house, then purchase the property without seeing it. Don't fall in love with a home. This is the best way to end up paying more than you would have because you have decided you "must" have it.

Conversely, sellers who are thinking with their emotions can give you the best hints on how motivated they are. For example, when someone says "I just want out" or "Please take it off my hands" or "I'm drowning in bills"—these are all terrific cues to you that you will be able to buy the property at a great discount.

Direct Contact Sources for Real Estate Properties

Real estate brokers and agents: These people are the ones "in the know." They see properties that have come onto the market all the time, and a relationship with as many real estate professionals as possible will help you keep your pulse on the industry.

Mortgage brokers: Many times people who are trying to get out of their homes will contact mortgage brokers to see if the broker will purchase their property. You may have to pay a commission or fee, but mortgage brokers are a good resource for finding motivated buyers and sellers.

Attorneys: All types of attorneys are good contacts because they are dealing with the issues that cause people to need to sell their homes. For example: divorce, bankruptcy, tax situations, lawsuits, etc. You want attorneys to think of you when one of their clients needs to sell a property quickly.

Financial experts: CPAs and financial planners make recommendations to their clients all the time regarding buying and selling real estate for tax and investment purposes. By developing a relationship with these professionals, you will be on their list when they recommend real estate to their clients.

Title Companies/Escrow Agents: These people work in the real estate industry each day and they record the details of each real estate deal. The nice thing about working with escrow agents or title companies is that the information they deal in is public record, so it is easy and legal for them to let you know of any distressed properties that come across their desks.

Lenders: You can contact loan managers at banks to let them know about your service. A person who is trying to get rid of a property quickly will contact his or her banker looking for help or an extension on a loan or line of credit. Bankers like to have someone to refer their clients to, because they don't have to tell clients they can't do anything to help them. Make sure they have your name and number as a referral source.

Other direct contact sources that you might consider networking are builders and contractors, rental property owners, and insurance agents.

Finding Properties

When selecting properties to consider for purchase, keep in mind two things: type of property and location. These two things will affect the amount of appreciation you will earn on the property.

They will also affect the selling price and the type of buyer or renter you will be able to attract.

The "right" location is defined by what you want. Neighborhoods, freeway access, schools, and price will all determine whether the property is right for what you want. You just need to determine your priorities and what you want out of the property. Here are a few guidelines that will help you stay away from less-appealing properties.

- Try to stay away from properties that need a significant amount of work, such as foreclosures that have been totally stripped or practically destroyed.

- A good home size to focus on is a three- or four-bedroom home. Focus mainly on residential properties. Almost all real estate properties are residential, and they are the ones that are easiest to move.

- Avoid really old homes. Try to purchase homes that are less than twenty years old. Older homes typically have outdated systems and require major work to bring them up to date and sometimes into compliance with code. Think about how much it would cost to replace the entire heating and cooling systems, plumbing and electrical systems, and pay to have asbestos or lead paint removed.

- Look for homes located in neighborhoods that are appreciating in value. Demand in an area is the number one reason for a home to appreciate, so look for areas that are "hot."

- Avoid areas that have rundown homes, high crime rates, and gang activity. Homes with poorly kept yards and broken-down cars in the same street are red flags to stay away from homes for sale nearby.

- Look for homes away from freeways, highways and busy streets—these are more appealing to buyers.

Where to Look

"For sale by owner" and distressed properties are a great starting point. Many FSBO (for sale by owner) properties become desperate because they don't want to pay an agent. They do not get as much exposure as those listed by agents, and therefore are usually motivated. Also, private and government auctions are another way to find deeply discounted properties.

Visit and research your county courthouse. Many properties have been seized for failure to pay taxes, and you can own them by simply paying the taxes owed. By spending several hours a week doing this type of research, you can hit pay dirt when you find such properties.

You can get a list of foreclosures through the Veterans Administration, the Federal Housing Administration, and the Department of Housing and Urban Development. This will help you to zero in on those distressed properties that you can purchase for 10-20% below market value.

The classified section in the newspaper lists hundreds of properties that are for sale, and whether they are FSBO or listed with an agent. Real estate agency magazines are another great source to locate homes. You can find them at most grocery stores and convenience stores for free. These typically list the price, features, and a picture of each of the properties being listed by that agency. There are many FSBO magazines of this type as well, that provide homeowners the same exposure for a fee. FSBO properties are usually easy to spot just by driving around the neighborhoods that interest you.

Evaluate the Property

The second step you must take after finding a property is to find out if it will bring in the desired profit. The easiest way to do this is by figuring out if the expenses are less than the income. If you determine a property will sell for $150,000, but buying it and fixing it up will cost you $145,000, you need to decide if $5,000 is enough of a profit for the effort.

One way to determine the value of a property is to look at "comps" in the surrounding area. Comparable properties that have sold recently can give you a ballpark of what your property could potentially net. A good Web site to use is www.zillow.com. The site offers great information as well as 3-D maps of properties. Once you have determined what the property could sell for, inspect the property and determine what repairs are needed in order to sell. Think about the location of the property and projected appreciation. Is the home right next to railroad tracks? If so, the appreciation on such a property will be less than a quiet home in a cul-de-sac. These are all issues that will help you determine if it is "worth" it.

Financial Equations to Use

A concept you must understand if you want to be successful in real estate investing is the time value of money. The basis of this concept is that you compare the value of a dollar today with the value of that dollar at some time in the future. A dollar is worth more now than if you receive it in the future.

You need to calculate how much you should pay for the asset when you buy it "today" versus how much your return will be in the future. This calculation is known as the "present value" of money.

By discounting the amount you want to receive in the future, you can arrive at the amount you want to pay today. Inflation can greatly affect the present value of a property and must be taken into account.

Appreciation is the increase in the value of your property. You can figure this out in dollars and then convert it to a percentage of the total. Calculating the appreciation on the property is a must, so that you can see what each property is netting you. For example, my home was purchased in 1990 for $100,000 and sold ten years later for $150,0000. The appreciation on the property is $50,000. Since I owned it for ten years, the average appreciation per year is $50,000 divided by 10, or $5,000. To determine the percentage, I take the appreciation that was earned ($50,000) and divide it by the purchase price or $100,000. This comes to .5 or 50%. Then I can figure the average per year by dividing our percent appreciation by ten years, and I come up with 5% per year.

So by doing this calculation, I can see that, over the course of the time I owned my home, I made an average of 5% of appreciation or $5,000 every year that I owned the house. Computing appreciation can quickly show you how holding a property for however long a period can make you money without your doing anything. Another thing to keep track of is the amount of principal that is paid on the loan during the course of the mortgage. This is called principal reduction and it increases the amount of equity in the property.

Using the same example—in ten years, I have paid $10,000 worth of the $100,000 principal on the mortgage. The principal reduction is $10,000. Now, when I sell my property for $150,000, I owe only $90,000 to the bank, so I net $60,000 of total equity on the transaction. By adding the principal reduction ($10,000) to the equity earned on the sale of the property ($50,000), I come up with my total equity of $60,000.

Once you have a total equity figure, you can calculate your equity return. Do this by taking your total equity of $60,000 and dividing it by the down payment on the property. In this example, we will say that I paid $10,000 for my down payment. Therefore, my equity return would be $60,000 divided by $10,000, which is 6 or 600%.

If you plan to rent a property you have purchased, a calculation you will want to make is to compute cash flow. You can do this by taking the total income minus the total expense. Obviously, if your expenses are more than the income, the cash flow will be negative. You want to stay away from negative cash flow because it is literally money out of your pocket.

Income is the money you receive in the form of rent. Expenses are things like—the mortgage payment on the property, taxes, depreciation, maintenance, insurance, and other expenses associated with your business such as cell phone, supplies, etc. Remember, just because you calculate a positive cash flow before you buy the property, that doesn't mean it couldn't turn around very easily.

Suppose you calculated the cash flow on 100% occupancy. What happens when half of your tenants move out and their units are sitting vacant? Suddenly your income has been reduced by half and your expenses remain where they were when you figured your cash flow. You must be careful with this situation. You don't want to end up as a "motivated" seller yourself!

Physical Evaluation

After you've completed all the calculations, you should still evaluate the property physically. If possible, visit the property and see the location as well as the overall condition. Make a general decision about whether the property will fit with your overall investment strategy.

Take some time to do an initial inspection of the property. Start outside and measure the house. Look at the condition of the curbs, sidewalk, driveway, and the exterior. Check the roof, doors, windows, and screens, as well as gutters and downspouts. Remember, not everything has to be perfect; you are looking for red flag items. Don't forget to check the foundation for cracks and any wood (such as decks or patios) for termite or water damage. Notice if there is a fence and its condition.

Next, move inside and check the appliances, air conditioner, furnace, and water heater. Look at the floors, walls, electrical fixtures, and plumbing. Don't forget to notice things like closets and storage space. Take note of the layout of the house and the number of bedrooms. Does it have an open floor plan or is it cramped and dark? Think like a buyer. Would you want to live there? Check other features such as a pool, fireplace, etc.

Now that you have figured the math and visited the property, find out what kind of financing is already in place. Talk to the owner about the current arrangement. Find out if there has been an appraisal done on the house, and when it occurred. Talk to real estate agents or other homeowners in the neighborhood to find out more about the neighborhood itself. Check out any recent sales in the neighborhood to develop a list of comparable listings. This will help you get a general idea about the property values in the area. Lastly, you can also obtain the assessed tax value from the property appraiser's office.

Once you have made these three evaluations, you should be able to make an educated decision about whether the property is appropriately priced and whether or not you want to invest in it. Here is a property visit checklist that you can take with you when inspecting a property.

- House Measurements
- Landscaping condition
- Curbs
- Sidewalks and driveway
- Exterior (paint, siding, stucco) and condition
- Roof
- Doors and Windows (screens)
- Gutters and Downspouts
- Foundation
- Decks, Patios (rot, termite damage)
- Fence
- Condition of appliances
- Floors and Walls
- Electrical fixtures and wiring
- Plumbing
- Closets and storage
- Layout of home
- Number of bedrooms
- Type of insulation
- Additional amenities (pool, fireplace, etc.)

Rental Properties — Apartment and Condos

Many investors are looking for rental properties to purchase and hold. You can often utilize single-family residential homes as rental units, but often an apartment complex, duplex, fourplex, or condominium is a great way to bring in rental income.

When evaluating rental property (or income property), you can use the gross rent multiplier (GRM) in order to quickly decide if the property is worth investigating further. Each area has a different GRM, and you can find out what it is by contacting a real estate broker in that area. When you multiply the GRM by the gross rental income of the property, you can determine its value. Let's look at an example to clarify this concept.

Suppose we are looking at investing in a ten-unit building where the rent on each unit is $500 and the GRM in this specific area is 4. Ten units times $500 per month equals $5,000 per month in gross rental income (GRI). Multiply the monthly GRI of $5,000 by twelve months, and you get $60,000 per year in GRI for the property. The value of the property is then determined by multiplying GRI by GRM, which in this case is $240,000.

Determining the value of a rental property this way is only a means to an end. Once you have quickly figured the property value, you can better determine if it is a great deal or a lousy deal. Looking back at our example, we determined that the property value is $240,000. If the seller were asking $300,000 you would probably want to do more digging to find out why the asking price is so high. Is the building made of high-quality materials? Is there additional land or property included in the sale?

If the asking price on this same property is $200,000, you will probably want to move quickly to get that property under your control so that you can evaluate it and make your investment if it turns out to be a great deal.

Remember, the GRM method of determining value is really just a "quick and dirty" method of calculating value. It doesn't figure in operating expenses or financing concerns, so be careful.

Another method you can use to quickly evaluate a rental or income property is the cash on cash method. In this formula, you can figure out the return on your investment so that you can determine if it is a better investment than other options. You should do this with each real estate investment possibility to see if your money would be better invested elsewhere.

To calculate the cash on cash formula, you divide the projected net operating income (NOI) by the down payment. This will give you the amount of cash you have left after one year, expressed as a percentage of your original investment. Remember, the net operating income is the gross income less any operating expenses. Let's take a look at an example.

The property you are investing in has a net operating income of $1,000, and you can obtain the property with a $10,000 down payment. $1,000 divided by $10,000 equals 0.1 or 10%—which means you will make 10% on your investment of $10,000.

If you do similar cash on cash computations on other rental properties and find one that brings in NOI of $2,000 for your same down payment, the return would be 20% and would, on paper, be a better investment of your $10,000.

When evaluating condominiums, you can use a formula called price per foot per unit. Comparable condos in the area will list a price per foot per unit, and you can use this figure to compare the property you are evaluating. To calculate the price per foot per unit for your unit, simply divide the price of the unit by the square footage of that unit. For example, if the condominium price is $60,000 and contains 1,200 square feet, then the price per square foot per unit would be $60,000 divided by 1,200 or $50/sf/unit.

Now that we have talked about ways to determine whether rental properties can be a good value, you should take into consideration the following factors to make a better decision.

Vacancy Rate: If you forget to include this in your calculations, what you thought was a good investment could come back to bite you. For many properties, the average vacancy rate is 5%; in other words, 5% of the units will be vacant during the year. However, you want to make sure to get the actual rental records for a few years to determine what the true vacancy rate is for that particular property. Some properties can have vacancy rates as high as 25%. By looking at the actual records, you can determine just how consistent and continuous the income stream is for the property you are evaluating.

Property Management: Rental units need management; usually onsite, and you will want to ensure the current system is working well. If it is not, you will need to replace it or change the system.

Operating Costs: Are the units metered individually so that the tenants are responsible for their own utilities? Is the property owner responsible for all utilities? Paying the utilities can add a great deal to the operating costs of the property, and if this is the case, you must add this in to your evaluation of the deal. You can also find out ahead of time, how much it would cost to have each unit metered separately. This would constitute a one-time outlay of funds, but in the long run, it may significantly reduce the operating costs of the property.

Property Maintenance: Find someone you can trust, and then make a deal to share the profits or pay the person a monthly fee. Think about whether you want to be awakened at two o'clock in the morning to fix a plugged toilet. If you can find one person to handle all your maintenance and renovation/repair work, it can be a win-win situation for both of you. The contractor can make extra money on the side by doing odd jobs in your properties, and you have someone you can trust to handle the jobs you don't want to worry about.

Current Financing: Find out what financing is in place and what the current rate of interest is. The financial arrangements of a property could have a positive or negative effect on your evaluation.

Condition of Property: Evaluate the physical buildings carefully to determine what repairs or renovations will need to be conducted and when. Do the buildings have aluminum or vinyl siding that will not need painting? Have the units ever been renovated? Will the roof need to be replaced in ten years? By figuring out all of these issues ahead of time, you can build your offer around a realistic value of the property, as well as plan your operating budget to account for the future repairs that will need to be made.

Alterations: Can changes or improvements bring in more money in the form of additional rent? Does the property have large units that could be split into smaller ones, thereby doubling the occupancy rate? Can lofts be added to units with high ceilings, increasing the square footage of those units and justifying an increase in the monthly rent payment? Can a laundry facility be added to the property that could bring in $60-$90 per month in additional income? Other amenities can be added that would justify a higher rent. An investor should consider all of these things when looking to purchase rental property to hold.

Distressed Sales/Motivated Sellers

When the economy has downturns, such as after 9/11, many people lose their jobs as companies scramble to stay solvent. Due to this and increasing amounts of consumer debt, bankruptcy and foreclosure numbers are skyrocketing. Foreclosure rates most recently have set records in several states due to an increase in mortgage loan defaults and the sub-prime market crash.

There are several reasons why a property is being foreclosed upon. Usually, it is because of a major change in the homeowner's financial situation such as the loss of employment or a major medical crisis. In today's market, one of the main reasons for foreclosures is that people are defaulting on their loans. Many homebuyers bought their homes when the market was booming and there were many loan options. Most people were able to buy a home without any down payment and they were also offered loans with teaser rates. Now that these teaser rates are adjusting, people are finding it hard to make their monthly mortgage payments since their payments in most cases have more than doubled. What is even worse is that these people can no longer refinance their homes since lenders have made borrowing guidelines a lot stricter. Those who do qualify for a refinance, find themselves having no equity in their homes and having their homes appraised at values that are usually lower than when they first bought their homes. In some ways, this might be one of the greatest times to get into real estate investing due to a huge supply of homes on the market without much demand.

Usually, banks and lenders try to do all they can to keep from foreclosing on a property. However, sometimes the situation becomes so severe that a foreclosure is the only option. Here are some reasons why a mortgage can go into default.

- Failure to make mortgage payments
- Failure to maintain insurance on the property
- Failure to pay property taxes
- Failure to pay liens on the property
- Failure to maintain the property in good condition
- Failure to comply with other conditions in the mortgage agreement

Not all properties are foreclosures, however. Distressed sale purchasing opportunities exist on several different levels. You can purchase a property from the homeowner before the lender repossesses the home. In this situation, the owners are very motivated to get anything out of the property rather than have a foreclosure on their credit report.

This is the ideal investment opportunity. First, you identify how much money is needed to stop the foreclosure action. Then you can approach the homeowners with the opportunity. You offer to pay the required amount and provide a lease for the homeowners to remain in the home, and, in exchange, the homeowners agree to deed the home to you. Let's go through the process step by step.

Step 1

You offer to pay whatever mortgage payments, taxes, etc. that are in arrears and begin making the monthly mortgage payments on the property. The homeowners win because the foreclosure action is stopped and their credit is saved.

Step 2

The homeowners deed the property to you. You now own a property for the small price of the defaulted payments (much less than the entire mortgage on the home).

Step 3

You enter into a lease agreement with the homeowners to allow them to stay in the home and begin making their monthly payments to you. This amount should be enough to cover the monthly mortgage to the lender that you are now paying, and a small administrative fee.

With people who are in a dire financial situation, you may be forced to wait longer than you would like to start receiving monthly payments. However, if you think about how much you are getting the property for, a few more mortgage payments in exchange for ownership is a small price to pay.

Step 4

You can provide your new tenants with a buy-back option that will allow them to purchase the property back from you at any time during the term of the lease. The amount to "buy back" the home should be twice what you originally paid to stop the foreclosure action plus any mortgage payments you had to "cover" without a payment from the tenant. For example, if you paid $10,000 to stop foreclosure action, plus paid $500 in mortgage payments for three months while your tenants got back on their feet. The buy-back amount should be $23,000 ($10,000 + $1,500 = $11,500 x 2 = $23,000).

This type of situation becomes a win-win situation for both you and the homeowners. It allows the homeowners to stay in their home and work through their financial difficulties, while maintaining their credit and escaping the threat of foreclosure. They also can rest easy that they can still buy their home back at a future date when their situation becomes better.

You win as well because you are able to purchase a property at a huge discount, and then receive a positive cash flow from the tenants. If they decide to buy back the property from you, you have doubled your original investment. If the homeowner never repurchases, then you still have purchased the property at a discount and now own it. Holding the property for an extended period can generate substantial returns in appreciation and equity.

Another level of distressed sale is purchasing the home while it is in the foreclosure process between homeowners and lender. You can also purchase an already foreclosed home from the lender.

Once a property has been foreclosed on, the ownership is transferred to the lender who holds the note on the property. When this happens, the property becomes known as real estate owned (REO) by the lender or bank. REO properties can usually be purchased at a substantial discount from the lender or purchased at an auction. Many times, the lender will provide some of the financing. Banks and lenders don't want to own homes, and they are very motivated to sell them once they have been forced to foreclose.

Finding properties that are nearing foreclosure or are already in the foreclosure process is quite easy. You can contact the Federal Housing Administration (http://www.fha.gov/) or the Department of Veterans Administration (http://www.va.gov) to get the names of real estate agents who can show you foreclosed properties.

Properties can also be purchased at auction from the government or a private holder. You can see a list of properties up for auction by the government at www.treas.gov. The properties can often be purchased at greatly discounted prices; however, make sure you learn everything you can about these properties in advance. Determine exactly how much you are willing to spend, and don't go over your limit. If you can get a "fixer-upper" for a great discount, then it is a great buy. You don't want to get caught up in the auction process and spend away your profits.

Be wise in purchasing these types of properties. Many homeowners, knowing they are going to lose their house, will strip everything of value out of the home before they leave it. Make sure you evaluate these properties before making any deals on them. You can find small businesses with whom to partner. Service companies with painters, plumbers, housecleaning services, repair people, electricians, etc. may work a deal with you to handle all of your repairs when their employees would otherwise be idle. With creative thinking, you can benefit all parties.

The great thing about discount buying is that the profit margin is much higher and can be shared. You can use bartering to find services you will need for those "fixer-upper" properties. Find a repair person or contractor who can partner with you or receive a percentage of the deal. This way, even if you know nothing about home repair, you can still fix up the properties that need it, increasing the eventual selling price that much more.

By taking advantage of distressed properties that have already been retuned to the lien-holder (the lender), you can structure your deals to make a profit as well as sell the property at a discount to someone who might not otherwise be able to afford it.

Types of Financing

Conventional Mortgages

Conventional mortgages are the most difficult to assume and obtain. If you are buying many different properties to use as rentals, most lending institutions will stop providing conventional loans because of your increased risk for negative cash flow from vacancy and delinquent rent payments. Additionally, conventional mortgages give you no control over the payment schedule or the interest rate, as the lender dictates these. Most likely, you will want to avoid conventional mortgages in most cases.

Block Financing

Block financing allows you to use a combination of mortgages to ease the transaction and reduce the down payment.

Existing Loan Assumption

Assuming a loan means that you keep the original property owner's existing loan in place and merely begin making the payments. You assume all of the seller's rights and obligations under the original mortgage loan. As mentioned above, you do not want to assume a conventional mortgage. There are a couple of other situations where you would want to put together new financing rather than assume the existing loan. These are in the case of a loan where the mortgage balance is low, say less than 40% of the total mortgage. This gives you so little leverage that it is not worth assuming the loan. When assuming a mortgage, look for loans with 40-100% of the mortgage remaining.

Another situation where you would not want to assume a loan is if the interest rate on the existing loan is high. A good number to use when determining whether or not the interest rate is competitive is 3%. If the existing loan interest rate is more than 3% above the going market interest rate, do not assume the loan. It will cause your mortgage payments to be prohibitively high and will greatly reduce your profits.

Seller-Owned Note

This type of financing occurs when the sellers would rather receive a monthly payment instead of one lump sum on the purchase of their property. This most often occurs when people are reaching retirement age and have already paid off the mortgage on their home (or are close). Instead of receiving the entire amount to sit in the bank earning 3%, these sellers would rather act as the mortgaging institution and receive a monthly payment with interest from the buyer. In this situation, the sellers are actually investing their property's equity with you and receiving a better interest rate than if they put the entire amount in the bank. It also assures them a certain monthly income as other regular income sources dwindle or cease.

Sometimes these sellers won't want to make their "mortgage" with you for as long as thirty years. In these cases, you would simply arrange for a balloon payment, or payment of the remaining balance, at the end of whatever period they want for the arrangement. When this final payment comes due, you can arrange for other financing at that point, or sell the property.

Second Mortgage

Second mortgages can be used to limit your down payment amount. A second mortgage can be used on primary residences as well as investment properties. It will typically have an interest rate higher than the first mortgage and a term of only ten to fifteen years. The mortgage company will use a ratio to determine the maximum it is willing to lend. In the case of a second mortgage, make sure there is not an automatic acceleration clause that can allow the balance of the loan to become payable in full immediately.

Single Payment Mortgage

A single payment mortgage is a loan that requires one payment at the end of the term. The one and only payment includes all principal and interest. The term is typically five to seven years. Sellers may be interested in this type of financing because it helps them avoid capital gains taxes for the length of the mortgage and allows ALL of the interest to accumulate before they receive it. This can be a very important and useful type of financing.

Sale-Leaseback

As discussed earlier, a sale-leaseback arrangement allows sellers to transfer ownership to you, while then leasing back the right to remain in the home. This is typically used when homeowners have not found another home or are building a home that has not been completed. You gain control of the property, and they don't have to move to an apartment or other rental until their next residence is available.

Joint Venture

Another type of financing involves entering a joint venture with the seller. This typically occurs when sellers have built up significant equity in the property and do not necessarily want to sell, but need cash flow. What you can do is to enter a joint venture with the sellers to purchase a portion of the equity in the property while they retain ownership. You pay them for this percentage of equity.

Shared Appreciation Mortgage

In a shared appreciation mortgage, the sellers accept a lower selling price in exchange for a portion of the equity when the home is sold at a future date. For example, if I want to sell my home for $200,000 but I need to get out of it quickly, I can sell it to you for a reduced price of $180,000. In exchange for the discounted price, you agree to pay me a portion of the equity that has increased when you sell the home two years down the road for $220,000. A variation of this is called an equity kicker, and it eliminates the up-front outlay of capital by receiving it later when the home is sold.

Short-Term Seller Financing

In this type of financing, the seller agrees to provide the financing on the property for a short period, usually six to twelve months. This is a great way to use other people's money to control the property until it can be repaired and resold at a profit. It makes the seller a money partner with you. This is a good method to use if you are going to find a buyer quickly for the property and then "flip" it.

Equity Cash-Out Refinancing

By refinancing a property after it has been purchased, the equity in the home is effectively transferred from seller to buyer.

Notes as Down Payment

Another way to come up with a down payment on a property purchase is to use a note from a previous transaction as the down payment instead of cash. The seller receives the note on another property giving him or her control of the equity in that property.

Wrap-Around Mortgage

In this type of financing, the sellers continue to make the mortgage payments on their existing loan, but the investor pays the sellers from the proceeds of the new loan. This is a good way to take advantage of a loan with very favorable terms or an interest rate that is not assumable. An example would involve buyers looking for a certain type of home, and they are willing to pay you $600 a month in rent. If you can find a distressed property and structure the financing so that you make the existing mortgage payments of

$450 per month, you are netting $150 a month in positive cash flow by "wrapping" the new mortgage "around" the old one.

Installment Purchase

This type of financing is similar to buying an appliance at a department store. The purchase price and even the down payment can be split into several payments over time. This gives the investor time to fund the transaction.

Note with Balloon Payment

The majority of the balance on the loan is due in one lump sum at a future date. The note promises this payment at the end of the term. This type of financing also gives the investor time to put together the financing needed for the purchase.

First and Second Note

This method splits the purchase price into two notes, a first note and a second note. The seller can hold the second note for cash flow.

Cash Flow Mortgage

This type of financing would be arranged on a rental property where you know exactly what the incoming cash flow will be. You set up the payment on the loan to match the cash flow from the rental. This way, you can assure that the incoming cash flow is the same as the mortgage payment on the property.

Land Contracts

This could be called a "buyer lease" because the seller retains the title to the property until the full purchase price has been paid. However, during the term of the note, the buyer has full use of the property.

Negative Amortization

The monthly payments for the first several years are less than the total amount of interest owed. Nothing is paid on the principal, and it actually increases as more interest is accumulated. The lower payments at first allow the buyer to qualify for a bigger loan. Also known as a buy down, you can purchase the interest rate down for the first few years to keep the payment low.

Using these different types of financing, you want to choose the mortgage option that has the lowest monthly payment and the quickest payoff. You must ensure the seller will agree to the methods you wish to use. The five most common payoff options are amortized mortgages, balloon payments, interest-only mortgages, negative amortization mortgages, and single-payment mortgages.

You can also combine different financing types to meet the unique needs of each transaction. If you are creative in your thinking, you can meet the needs of both seller and buyer, all the while making a profit for you and your money partners.

The Basics of a Real Estate Deal

Opening the Deal

Once you have identified a potential seller, and have made an appointment to get specifics, your next step in the transaction is to evaluate the property and the details of the transaction to determine the risk involved. In the appointment, you will need to get information from the seller so you can properly evaluate the deal. Here is a checklist of information you will need.

Seller

- Name
- Address
- Phone Number
- Time and Place to Call

Property

- Location of Property (street, city, state)
- Type of Property
- Description of Property
- Improvements Made?

Property Sale

- Date of Sale
- Selling Price
- Down Payment Amount
- Amount of First Mortgage
- Amount of Second Mortgage (if any)
- Current Property Value and Basis for Valuation

Mortgage

- Date of Mortgage
- Original Mortgage Amount
- Terms in Months
- Interest Rate
- Payment Amount
- Date of First Payment
- Next Payment Due Date
- Balloon Payment (if any) and Due Date
- Number of Payments Left Owing
- Current Balance of All Loans Secured by the Property

After you have the information you need from the seller, your next step is to take care of your due diligence. There are three "P's" that make up the due diligence you will need to perform when working on a deal. They are paperwork, property, and people.

Paperwork: With every real estate transaction, there are certain documents that you must request to have the information you need to evaluate the deal.

- Mortgage promissory note
- Mortgage or deed of trust
- Closing statement
- Fire and hazard insurance policy
- Title insurance policy
- Title search
- Current loan's amortization schedule

Property: The things you will need for the second "P" will help you determine the actual value of the property you are purchasing.

- Appraisal of property
- Photographs of property
- Property description and improvements made since last sale
- Map showing location

People: The people you are most concerned about are those who will be buying or renting from you. Make sure you always qualify your buyers and renters to reduce your own risk.

In handling the due diligence phase of the deal, make sure you pay attention to the details. By doing your job thoroughly, you can earn a reputation as a competent professional in the industry. Shoddy attention to details can ruin your credibility and cost you money on unwise business transactions.

Leverage and Financing

One of the important concepts to understand when creating financial deals is the concept of leverage. Leverage is the percent/amount of other people's money that you use in your investments. If you invest $100 of your own money in a CD or stock, you have zero leverage. You have used your own money. However, in almost every real estate transaction there is some leverage used. Even when the average homeowners buy a home as a primary residence, they have used leverage because they take out a loan for the majority of the purchase price. They paid the down payment out of their own pockets and the lending institution pays the rest. You can compute leverage using the following calculations: increase in property value divided by cash down payment amount.

If you are able to buy a property without using your own money, then the cash down payment amount is zero. As we all learned in grade-school math, you cannot divide by zero. In this case, the return on your investment can be infinite. You can figure your return on investment from appreciation, principal reduction, taxes, or cash flow by dividing by the cash down payment. Let's take a look at an example.

I purchase a property for $100,000 using $5,000 of my own money. I hold the property for three years, while renting it to tenants whose payment covers the mortgage payment. At the end of three years, the property has appreciated and is now worth $105,000. I have also used other people's money (the tenants') to pay the mortgage and have reduced the principal by $1,000 per year. So, by adding up the factors that increase the property value, I get $8,000 ($5,000 in appreciation plus $1,000 a year for three years). So to calculate my return on investment, I take $8,000 divided by $5,000 and I get 1.6 or 160%. Not a bad return at all!

Utilizing leverage does have its pitfalls however. The more leverage you use the greater your chance for profits, but it opens you up to potential risks. For example, you have $80,000 and you buy a property outright as a rental unit. In this case, you will have no mortgage payment since you have paid the entire price in cash. If your renter does not pay his or her rent or if the unit remains vacant, you are out nothing. Now consider another scenario. If you take the same $80,000 and buy ten properties using more leverage, you will have ten mortgage payments of $1,000 each. If four of those properties remain vacant, you are paying $4,000 a month of your own money to lenders. The greater your leverage the greater the potential for negative cash flow. However, the greater your leverage the greater your return on investment (ROI). Let's look at a few examples to illustrate this point.

Property Sale Price: $100,000
Increase in Value: $5,000

If you pay 100% of the price, you have zero leverage and your ROI is 5% or 5,000 divided by 100,000.

If you pay a $50,000 down payment or 50%, and leverage the other 50%, you now receive an ROI of 10% (5,000 divided by 50,000).

Going even further, if you pay only $25,000 as a down payment, which equates to 25%, and leverage the remaining 75%, then your ROI increases to 20% because 5,000 divided by 25,000 equals .20.

Finally, if you put a mere $10,000 down on the property (10%) and finance the rest, your return on investment is whopping 50% (5,000 divided by 10,000).

Get it in Writing

After you conclude the negotiations, you need to have all parties sign a contract to put the deal in writing. Contracts will protect all parties and will help you control your liability. A real estate contract is an agreement between the buyer and the seller that establishes the elements of the deal. It can be simple or complex, but it will be the one thing that will protect you from problems. The language in a real estate contract will protect you against fraud as well as simple unexpected issues that come up. Because you are dealing with someone you usually don't know very well, make sure your contracts are in order to protect him or her as well as yourself. A well-worded contract will make both parties more secure in the transaction.

Contracts contain certain terms that will help you to legalize the "deal." These terms are:

- Deed: The deed represents ownership. The person who possesses the deed owns the property.

- Promissory note: A promise to repay debt.

- Mortgage: Also called a deed of trust, this is the security or collateral used with the promissory note.

- Lease: Gives you the right to possess the property in exchange for a certain amount of money.

- Options: An agreement that gives you the right to purchase a property at a specified price within a certain amount of time in exchange for a fee paid to the seller.

Let's explore options more fully. They can be great tools when structuring a deal.

Options

One of the best devices to use when investing in real estate is the option agreement. This type of agreement gives you the right to purchase a property at a specified price within a specified time in exchange for a fee paid to the seller. This gives you the advantage of controlling a piece of real estate that you want to purchase without having to purchase it right away.

The use of an option agreement mainly gives you time to determine your strategy with the property. You can decide if you want to turn around and sell it or turn it into a rental property. It allows you to work with your partners to determine the best course of action, as well as to line up a buyer for the property if that is the way you decide to go.

You can also take advantage of the equity and appreciation that will build during the option period, thus making the property more attractive at the end of the period. It also helps you minimize your risks because you have not committed anything but the option fee. If you determine at the end of the option period that you do not want to purchase the property, you have lost only the fee.

If, by the end of the period, you have decided the deal is not going to result in a positive cash flow for you, then don't pursue the deal. If you are still unsure, you can extend the option for another fee. You need to build this choice into the original agreement. It allows you to extend the option for another period for another fee to the seller. Try to get as long an extension as possible for the lowest fee you can.

Another clause that many sellers will want included with the option is the right to keep the property on the market. Sellers will not necessarily want to wait while you put together your funding, and they may wish to keep their home on the market in case they get another, better offer. In this case, they would have thirty days to notify you that they have received another offer, and then you would be able to either match the new offer or cancel your original deal. This is usually not a good situation for what you are trying to accomplish, so try to exclude this option if possible.

Some other options you will want to consider with any purchase contract are assignment, applying rent to purchase, and the escape clause. When working with contracts, the more you can do to protect your interests, the better. The better you can tie up the property, control it, and then create an exit strategy for the property, the more profit you will make.

Assignment

Placing an assignment clause in your purchase contract allows you to assign the contract to another party or person. An example assignment clause would be "...to be purchased by John Doe and/or as assigned."

Applying Rent to Purchase

If you have tenants in a rental property who plan to purchase the property from you, you can insert a clause that will apply some percentage of their rent toward the final purchase price of the property. Commonly referred to as "rent to own," you determine what percentage of each month's rent will go toward a "down payment" on the purchase of the property.

Escape Clause

This is likely to be the most important option you can put in your contract. It states that you can be released from the deal if you find any problems during the inspection of the property. This is important because it will allow you to get out if the inspection shows there are major concerns with the property. You don't want to get stuck with a "money pit" that you weren't prepared for, so make sure you put an escape clause in place. An example escape clause is "This offer is subject to the inspection and approval of the property by they buyer prior to the transfer of possession."

When utilizing options on contracts, there are two things you need to remember to minimize your risk. The first is to always make sure the owner of the property has adequate insurance on the property. You don't want to spend a lot of time considering a property that could be subject to damage from the elements or accident.

Another thing to remember is to have the contracts recorded at the courthouse. This will protect you in case the owner tries to refinance the property or use it as collateral on another mortgage loan.

Having the contract signatures notarized is another form of protection. This will help your contract hold up legally if a dispute ever arises. Both you and the other party would have to prove your identities and show that you are signing the agreement of your own free will in the presence of a notary public.

Closing the Deal

After you have completed the due diligence, have determined the course of action, and structured the deal, you still must follow certain steps in order to close the transaction. The closing is the process of signing the documents to transfer the mortgage, and can be handled at an attorney's office or the office of a title company with which you had opened escrow. The title company you work with will usually give you a list of everything you need in order to close the deal. Work closely with your escrow agent and utilize that agent often, as the agent wants to close the deal as much as you do.

Chapter 5

Real Estate Notes

Once the decision is made to purchase a home, buyers must sort through the multiple requirements and options to find the ideal way to finance their purchase. Most people choose to apply for a loan from a bank. They can expect to be required to come up with a down payment of 2-25% of the selling price.

Once the down payment can be made, the bank will evaluate the buyers' credit and economic situation to determine if the buyers will be able to make payments on the home. Once the buyers provide the down payment and qualify for the remaining amount of the loan, they will sign the promissory note or a "note of hand." This is a written promise to pay, or repay, a specified sum of money at a stated time or on demand. This completed process forms a mortgage.

A mortgage binds the loan amount of the promissory note to the house. If the conditions of the promissory note are not met, the house can be taken by the bank and sold to fulfill the debt obligation. The promissory note is the actual debt, and the mortgage is the security on that debt.

In some cases, buyers cannot qualify for traditional methods of financing, and this means that sellers can be unable to find qualified buyers for their homes. One solution is "seller-baked financing" which allows the seller to provide for some or all of the financing. A new industry has been created to buy and sell shares of these privately held mortgages. This industry is known as real estate note buying.

Advantages of Seller-Backed Financing

- Buyers have more freedom from the rigid bank requirements such as making a specific down payment, meeting federal qualification criteria, closing delays, bank fees, and extensive paperwork.

- The sellers, not a bank, receive the interest.

- It provides flexibility for both the buyers and the sellers.

- Sellers can minimize the amount of the capital gains tax they would have to pay by doing the financing themselves.

- Sellers can receive a steady cash flow over a period of time, rather than a large amount in a single lump sum.

- Buyers have more flexibility in the amount they are required to come up with for a down payment.

- Buyers may be able to get a better interest rate than they could have gotten from a larger financial institution.

The only requirements for seller-backed financing to take place are that the sellers and the buyers meet to agree upon the terms of the final selling price, down payment, and interest rate. This form of financing is faster and easier to complete, and it minimizes the amount of paperwork needed.

Those who hold private mortgage notes will admit that it is a great way to safely invest their money; however, as time passes, the holders may find that they need to sell their notes to get money for other things. Perhaps they need to pay for a wedding, college, or medical expenses. It may just be that they would like to finance a vacation or they need the cash for another big purchase. A note holder may have lost his or her job and needs money. For whatever reason, there are always note holders who are looking to sell their mortgage notes. This business revolves around investors finding these private mortgage holders who want to sell their notes for less than the market value of the note.

Direct Contact Sources for Real Estate Notes

You can utilize the same direct contact sources as you would when looking for investment properties. In the previous chapter, we discussed building relationships in order to get solid leads. You can use the same sources such as real estate brokers, attorneys, financial advisors, and escrow agents in order to find those people in need of selling a privately held mortgage note. Here are few other direct contact sources.

Builders and Contractors

Many builders and contractors have a lot of money tied up in the property that they are building and are generally anxious to sell the property so they can start building more. This is a great source to look at for real estate notes at reduced prices. Since most builders need cash to continue working, they will welcome the chance to see a quick turnaround.

Rental Property Owners

Rental properties can be a great source to look because many times renting is a hassle for the owner. Receiving a bulk payment in exchange for the hassle can be a very persuasive offer. You can easily find rental property owners in the newspaper.

Insurance Agents

Since insurance agents are constantly helping people to get homeowners insurance on their homes, they are a great source to look to for referrals. You can help the insurance agents by recommending their services to note buyers and sellers in exchange for referrals on home or property owners.

Mortgage Note Structure

It is important to become familiar with the basic structure of the mortgage note. There are seven categories that are typically included in any mortgage note, and each of these is fundamental in protecting the rights of those involved and the value of the property. The categories that we will discuss are the introductory clause, interest clause, covenants and representations of the mortgagor clause, damage and destruction clause, junior financing clause, assignment clause, and default clause.

The introductory clause is found at the beginning of the note. It is used to define all parties who will be involved in the purchase of the note. It also provides the basic amounts and general terms tied to that amount, including a brief description of the property that is involved in the transaction. Just as an introduction to a book gives a brief overview of what is to come, so does the introductory clause, which "introduces" the parties and terms involved in the sale.

The interest rate clause defines what the interest rate will be and how it will be paid. This includes the type of interest rate, fixed or variable. A fixed interest rate remains at the same value throughout the course of the loan; whereas, a variable interest rate adjusts the percentage of interest to the course of the economy, for example, the prime rate plus 4%. This will fluctuate with whatever index of interests that banks use to set their interest rates. You can check out current market rates on various index rates at www.bankrate.com.

The covenants and representations of the mortgagor clause basically define the set of rules for the mortgage. This clause sets the amount of the loan balance and the amount the borrower will pay for interest. This clause also includes how taxes and assessments will be paid. It will also list the requirements for the borrower to ensure proper maintenance on the property and to carry homeowner's insurance. The covenants and representations of the mortgagor clause are basically a safeguard for the person buying the note to ensure that the borrower knows and fulfills all of his or her responsibilities.

The damage and destruction clause is designed to ensure that the value of the property remains at an appropriate level. It clearly defines the borrower's responsibilities in maintaining the upkeep of the property, as well as what is required if the property were to be damaged. It also states how much time is allowed for the damage to be recorded. Again, this clause protects the buyer of the note from purchasing an investment tied to an asset that no longer has value due to damage or destruction. By requiring the borrower to maintain the property, the value of the asset guaranteeing the note is upheld.

The junior financing clause protects the value of the property in comparison to the amount due on the note. This clause sets the rules for additional loans in which the property could be collateral. It also ensures that the primary lender will be the first one paid off if there are any problems. This clause also verifies that the note will not be secondary to another loan on the same property. This is another protection for the buyer, ensuring that the borrower does not use the property as collateral on another loan without maintaining the note as the primary. This means that any other debt incurred will be secondary to the note that was purchased.

The assignment clause provides the lender with protection from three areas of possible loss on the note. The assignment clause clarifies the options open to the lender in the case of condemnation of the property, if another party takes responsibility for payment of the note, or if the borrower rents out the property held by the note.

The default clause clearly defines the requirements of both parties and states the options that can be taken in the event that a violation of the contract occurs. The default can occur if any part of the contract is violated and an acceptable solution is not presented and agreed upon. This clause provides the lender with more security in investing in the note.

In this next section, we will discuss the time value of money and financial equations that will help you to determine whether or not a note is an investment worth making. In Appendix A, there are other equations and examples that may help you to understand these concepts more clearly.

The True Value of Money

The first thing you need to understand before you can begin any investment opportunity is how money operates. It is important to note the difference that can be made when investing money rather than letting that money suffer under the rate of inflation. Once you have a clear understanding of the difference between the two, you will be able to invest your money and receive the greatest financial gain.

The time value of money is the comparison between the value of a dollar today and the value of the same dollar in the future. Since you will be investing cash today to receive cash in the future, it is important to understand how time will change the value of your money. The standard notion is that the value of today's dollar is worth more than the future dollar. For example, $1,000 earned today and held in a safe would decrease in value over time. This is further illustrated in the table below. It shows the correlation between the amount of time money is kept versus the average amount of inflation over the years. As you can see, $1,000 sitting in a safe over time decreases in value. The higher the inflation rate the greater the rate of depreciation.

Year	3%	5%	7%
1 year	970.87	952.38	934.58
3 years	915.14	863.84	816.30
5 years	862.61	783.53	712.99
10 years	744.09	613.91	508.35

To utilize time as a benefit to your money, you must invest in assets that will increase in value. The real estate notes that you buy will increase in value each year. It is important to know how much the asset should be purchased for today, in order to receive the desired future return. Knowing how much your initial investment should be is the first of three steps in determining how long it will take to earn your desired gain. The other steps, which we will discuss in further detail later, are the risk level that you are willing to take and how long you are willing to invest your money. With these amounts determined, you will be able to search for notes that are specific to your desired goals.

When the initial investment combines with time and interest, a new concept is created. This is the concept of growing money, which is also known as compounding. The basic idea behind compounding is this: you have a predetermined amount of money that you invest, you gain a return on the money that you invested, and you turn around and reinvest the original money with the amount gained for a set amount of time. As you continue to do this, your base investment increases, which in turn leads to an increase in the amount of interest earned. For example, if you were to begin your investment with $1,000 at 7% interest, and you continue to grow your money, the result will be as follows:

Year	Original Amount		Interest Earned		Total Value of Investments
1	$1,000.00	+	$70.00	=	$1070.00
2	$1,070.00	+	$74.90	=	$1,144.90
3	$1,144.90	+	$80.14	=	$1,225.04
4	$1,225.04	+	$85.75	=	$1,310.79
5	$1,310.79	+	$91.76	=	$1,402.55

Doubling Your Money

So you may still be asking yourself how long it will take for you to be able to double your money. There is a shortcut used in the financial industry to determine how long it will take. This shortcut is called the "rule of 72." The rule of 72 states that all you need to do to determine how long it will take to double your money is to divide 72 by the percentage of interest that you will be earning. For example, if you were earning 8% interest, you would divide 8 into 72 and discover that it will take nine years to double your money. If you earn 12% interest, then it will take you six years to double your money.

Part of the time factor of the note is to evaluate the length of time that the note has been established. This includes evaluating how many payments have already been made on the note, the principal amount of the mortgage, and the present value of the note.

The Risk Involved

The final factor to consider when investing your money is the level of risk associated with the investment. Generally the higher the risk, the higher the potential gain will be. After learning a few simple formulas and identifying a few basic factors, you will be able to determine the amount of possible risk on each note. The risk factors and formulas to know are:

- loan-to-value ratio
- investment ratio
- type of property that secures the note
- creditworthiness of the person making payments on the note
- the appraised value of the property that secures the note

Let's go over each of these issues so you can see how these factors will help you to determine whether or not a note is going to be a worthy investment for you.

The Loan-to-Value Ratio (LTV)

To determine how secure the note is, you will need to use the loan-to-value ratio. This ratio compares the amount due on the loan against the value of the property that guarantees the note. From a lender's perspective, a high LTV mortgage is more risky than one in which the LTV is low. When the LTV is high, the borrower can expect to pay a higher interest rate. Borrowers with less equity in a property have less to lose, which puts lenders more at risk.

This ratio can be identified by taking the sum of the outstanding balance on the loan divided by the appraised value of the property multiplied by 100. For example, if the property is appraised at $225,000 and the mortgage note amount is $180,000, then the LTV would be 80% ($180,000 / $225,000 = .80).

Investment to Value Ratio (ITV)

The second important formula to know and understand for note buyers is the investment-to-value-ratio. The ITV ratio is needed only if there are other liens against the property that would be senior to the note. This ratio determines the risk of the lender as compared to the value of the property when other liens are already in existence and would take seniority in the case of default on the note.

The formula is figured by first adding the principal balances of the senior liens on the property to the amount that is being invested for the note. Only the principal balance on senior liens is used, since liens that are junior to the note are not considered a risk. Once the sum of the balances is found, divide the amount by the property value. For example, if the property is worth $225,000 and the mortgage note amount is $180,000 and the senior liens have a sum of $20,000, then the investment to value ratio would be 88.9% ($180,000 + $20,000 = $200,000 / $225,000 = .888 * 100 = 88.9%)

Type of Property

The type of property that secures the note also helps to determine the risk factor. The percent acceptable for your LTV ratio depends on what type of property the note is secured by. The more long-term value the property holds for the owner, the higher the LTV ratio. If the note is secured by unimproved land, the LTV is the lowest. More middle-ground properties are those that are actively in use, but not by the owner. The most secure properties are residential properties where the owner resides in that property. If the note is secured with an unimproved piece of land, the LTV should not be above 50%. For commercial properties, the LTV can go up to 65%. Residential rental properties should stay below 70%, and for residential properties with the owner as the occupant, the LTV ratio can go up to 85%.

Credit History of the Payer

Always check the credit report of the person who will be making payments on the note. If the payer has had credit problems in the past, the funding source will need to know in order to properly determine the risk on the note. As part of the credit check, it is also important to check the employment history. These factors will give the funding source a good indication of the risk of the payee.

Appraised Value

The appraised value of the property is an amount determined by an unbiased professional known as an appraiser. There will be a small fee charged by the appraiser, but it is a small amount to pay to make sure that the funding source's money is secure. This value is a critical part of determining the risk factor, because this value is used in both LTV and ITV ratios.

Simultaneous Closings

A simultaneous closing occurs when the seller of a home agrees to carry the financing on the home and create a note. At the closing, the seller both creates the note and sells the note to a cash flow investor at a discount. This is called a simultaneous closing.

Why would a home seller want to do this? Many times, a seller does not want to offer seller financing and carry a note; he or she would rather just sell his house and pocket the cash. However, many times, a seller cannot do this for any one of several reasons.

- The seller needs to get out of the property quickly.
- The home has been on the market a very long time
- The property cannot be financed
- The buyer has trouble obtaining traditional financing

All of these reasons make it a good idea for a seller to offer seller financing in order to quickly sell the home. Because there are no stringent bank requirements to meet, the number of potential buyers who will be interested in the home will increase dramatically.

Because the seller in our "example" does not want to carry a note, but would rather have cash, he or she can agree to sell the note to an investor, at a discount. This can be done in a simultaneous closing, and the seller can get cash from the sale. If you can clearly explain this concept to sellers, you can both profit from the arrangement. Let's look at an example to clarify the concept.

John purchased a run-down home that was in terrible shape for $25,000. His intent was to get it at a "steal" and then fix it up for a profit. He borrowed $20,000 and made up the other $5,000 out of pocket. John then spent several months and $12,000 restoring the home. He had the interior and exterior painted, completely renovated the bathrooms and kitchen with new tile, counters, and fixtures, and had all new floor coverings installed throughout.

When he was finished with the renovations, the home had a fair market appraised value of $60,000. Once he was done with his remodeling, John wanted to sell the property quickly. He wanted his investment back so that he could move on to other investments. Due to the market being very slow, John decided to offer owner financing as an incentive to buyers.

After being inundated with potential buyers, John decided to sell to a young couple with stable jobs, but some past credit problems. They were motivated by the owner financing since they could not qualify for a traditional loan. John agreed to sell them the property for $60,000, with a $6,000 down payment due at closing.

The remaining $54,000 was in the form of a note, payable over thirty years at 11% interest. Because John wanted cash, not a monthly note payment, he agreed to a simultaneous closing and sold the note to an investor for $48,600. John will make a profit on the home, the buyers get into a home that they could not qualify for using traditional methods, and the note investor is able to invest in the note at a discount. Everyone wins!

The Basics of a Note Deal

Pre-Deal Evaluation

The first step that you need to take in your business as a note broker is to gather information. The information you will need to gather can be identified in five basic categories. These categories are seller information, property information, property sale information, mortgage note information, and background information. Listed below are the specific items to be gathered under each of the five categories of information.

Personal Information:
- First and Last Name
- Home Address
- Phone Number
- Other Contact Information

Property Information:

- Location
- Type (residential, rental, commercial, or unimproved land)
- Description (including improvements made to the property)

Property Sale Information

- Date of Sale
- Selling Price
- Amount of Down Payment
- Amounts of First and/or Second Mortgages
- Current Value of the Note
- What the Current Value is Based on

Mortgage Note Information

- Date of the Note
- Original Amount of the Note
- Terms of the Note in Months
- Interest Rate
- Payment Amount
- Date of First Payment
- Date of Next Payment
- Amount of Balloon Payment (if applicable)
- Number of Remaining Payments on the Note
- Current Balance of all Loans Secured by the Note

Background Information

- Payment History
- Credit History
- Seller's Motivation

Once you have collected as much of the data as you can, your next step will be to find the LTV ratio and the ITV ratio and then compare the percentages for the type of property that secures the note. The final step before determining whether you should try to make a deal is to look at the credit history of the borrower. It is not necessary to get a credit report at this point, but you will want to check on their payment history and employment information.

After completing the basic evaluation, you should have enough information to know if you would like to pursue the deal. If everything looks positive, you are ready to move onto the next stage, which is the actual formation of the deal, including the negotiation process.

Formation of the Deal

The responsibility of the note broker is to ensure that all paperwork is completed and that the deal is correctly evaluated. Using the information gathered in the pre-deal evaluation, you will be able to begin the negotiation process and form the actual deal. There are three main sections of information needed in the formation of a deal. These sections are the paperwork, the property, and the borrower. This process is a more in-depth evaluation based on the pre-note evaluation. Listed below are the specifics needed in each of the categories.

Paperwork

- Mortgage Promissory Note
- Mortgage or Deed of Trust
- Closing Statement
- Fire and Hazard Insurance Policy
- Title Insurance Policy
- Title Search

- Current Loan's Amortization Schedule
- An Estoppel Letter

Property

- Appraisal of the Property
- Photographs of the Property
- A Brief Description of the Property
- A Map of the Property

Borrower

- Credit Report
- Payment Record of Previous Payments Made on the Note

Gathering all of the information may take a little time, but doing a thorough job will ensure a better chance of success on the completion of the deal. Once you have the above information, you will need to review it with the funding source. Then you can begin the negotiation process. Once both parties have agreed, you are ready to close.

Closing the Deal

To close the deal, you will need to gather all of the paperwork needed and take it to an attorney's office or Title Company. Once there, all of the paperwork will be signed, and the mortgage will be transferred. You will need to verify that you have the eight documents listed above before you attempt to close the deal. Your escrow officer at the title company will also let you know if you need any additional documents or if anything is missing. Always use your escrow office for guidance or any questions you might have. Once you have completed these documents all that is left is for both parties to sign the paperwork and transfer the funds.

Financial Calculations

Below are a few examples of different calculations that you will probably run into. It is a good idea to know how to calculate different values when dealing with notes. You should consider investing in a business calculator if you don't already have one. A business calculator makes it is easy to solve for the amount that you will need to pay for the note in order to receive the profit desired.

Use the following key to know which amounts to enter.

N	I/Y	PV	PMT	FV
Number of Payments	Interest Per Year	Present Value of the Note	Amounts of the Payments	Future Value of the Note

Computing a Monthly Mortgage

Compute a monthly mortgage payment for a $90,000 loan at 8% interest for 25 years.

- N =300
- I/Y=8/12
- PV=$90,000
- PMT=?
- FV=$0

Answer: $694.63

Calculating the Present Value of the Mortgage Note

Figure out the reduced price that the above $90,000 mortgage note should be purchased for to receive 10% interest.

- N=300
- I/Y=10/12
- PV=?
- PMT=694.63
- FV=$0

Answer: $71,489.98

You can use your calculator to calculate other variables based on the situation.

Chapter 6

Factoring Invoices

One of the greatest growing segments of the financial industry is the area of purchasing business accounts receivable or invoices, also known as factoring.

The reason this is an expanding area is that many of today's businesses are working on tight budgets. They are required by business practice to grant terms to their customers. This means that after a company delivers its product or service, the customer then has up to three months to pay the bill.

In today's economy, many businesses can't wait long to receive the cash for their product. Companies need a consistent cash flow and do not want to see a huge balance in accounts relievable. The answer for these companies is factoring.

Factoring is the purchase of a company's invoices or accounts receivable at a discount for cash. The company receives cash, less the factor's fee, for the invoice. The buyer, or factor, benefits by receiving an investment that will turn over within thirty, sixty, or ninety days, and make a profit.

In the past few decades, businesses have come to rely on factoring to gain needed cash flow for growth and development, as well as regular operating expenses and overhead. Ironically, this well-used business tool is not taught in colleges, rarely mentioned in business plans, and is unknown to many in the business world. Factoring is an $80 billion dollar a year industry, and more and more small businesses are turning to factoring to maintain their cash flow.

How Factoring Works

Factoring is the process of purchasing commercial accounts receivable, or invoices, from a business at a discount. Factoring is different from financing because it is not a loan. Accounts receivable financing is when a bank uses a company's accounts receivable as collateral for a loan. In factoring, the factor actually purchases the debt instrument (invoice) from the business and pays them for it. The factor is then responsible for collecting on the invoice from the company's customer. The factor is paid for the invoice and receives a return on investment when it is paid. The factor receives the money he or she paid the company plus the profit from the discount purchase of the invoice.

Factors often provide other services to companies as well. In addition to providing cash that companies need to stay liquid and solvent, factors may also provide sales ledger and collection services, bad debt coverage or insurance against bad debts, and consultation. Factors will also ensure that the customer of the company have good credit before the company agrees to provide products or services.

Consultation by a factor can help businesses deal with unusual situations and navigate through the increasingly complex business world. Factors can charge a fee to provide expertise on financing possibilities and techniques to help the company increase its profits.

Companies today need cash flow, and banks do not provide the flexibility that many small companies want and need. Even using traditional methods of obtaining capital such as lines of credit, equipment leases, mortgages, and asset financing, a company can then become mired in debt. A high debt ratio can hobble a company and restrict its growth potential.

By using factoring, a company is not incurring new debt, since it is receiving cash from the assignment of an asset. It can be compared to selling a car. If you were to sell your car to someone in exchange for the car's market value, then you would end up selling an asset and receiving cash for it. This is a very simple example, but it explains the concept of the factor purchasing an asset from the company. The factor wins from this arrangement in that he or she is purchasing an asset without incurring debt. The invoice has already been filled, the factor merely has to wait until the terms of the invoice are up and take over the collection of the money. Look at the advantages that a company can benefit from when it factors its invoices:

- An immediate increase in capital/cash
- Factoring does not affect the company's credit rating
- More cash on hand to pay suppliers and bills
- No long-term contract and flexible terms
- The company can save on collection costs
- Better customer relations

Types of Factoring

There are two types of factoring available to use. These are recourse factoring and non-recourse factoring. The difference in these two types is who is responsible for the liability when a customer does not pay.

Recourse Factoring

In recourse factoring, the risk of non-payment remains with the company. If one of the company's customers fails to pay the factor, the company agrees to repurchase the invoice from the factor. The factor does not provide any protection to the company for a customer's failure to pay.

The factor can go back to the company if, for whatever reason, the invoice is not paid by the customer. Any debt resulting from a customer's failure to pay is reassigned to the company, and any money paid to the company by the factor can be demanded back by the factor.

Non-Recourse Factoring

In this type of factoring, the factor assumes the risk of non-payment. Once the invoice is purchased by the factor, the company is no longer responsible for any part of it. The factor is then responsible for collection of the money owed. The only situation where the company is not totally "divorced" from the process is if there is a dispute that arises over the quality of goods or services supplied by the company. In this case, the company would need to get involved to defend its position with the customer.

You may wonder why a factor would want to engage in non-recourse factoring when he or she must assume all the risk. There are actually several reasons. The first, and probably most apparent, is that companies are much more likely to sell invoices to a non-recourse factor. If a company is agreeing to sell its invoices, it doesn't want the bad debts coming back to haunt it. If the only invoices that the company must deal with are the non-paying ones, then a great deal of money is going to be spent trying to resolve these invoices, and it defeats the entire purpose of factoring business invoices in the first place.

Another reason why a factor would be willing to enter a non-recourse arrangement is that before the factor buys any invoices from a company, he or she has "due diligence" on the company's customers. The factor can perform credit checks to make sure the customers are credit worthy. He or she can also set a limit on the amount of credit the company can extend to any one customer. By limiting risk in this way, the factor can increase the chance that all of the invoices purchased from the company will be paid. By doing so, the company divests itself of the need to perform collections, and the factor is protected by limiting risk up front.

Another way a factor can protect himself or herself is to hold a certain percentage of the face value of a company's invoices in reserve. This is done so that if a problem arises regarding the goods or services performed, and the customer refuses payment, the factor can deduct that amount from the company's reserve amount.

Most of the investors who provide factoring are non-recourse factors. The investment returns from non-recourse factoring are much better and outweigh the protection from risk that a recourse arrangement would provide. In fact, in some states, recourse factoring can be considered a loan, and this subjects them to the usury laws of those states.

Confidential Factoring

In this type of arrangement, the company's customers are not aware that the factor is the one receiving their payment. This arrangement can be made with both recourse and non-recourse factoring. The customer is simply unaware of the collector pf the invoice payment.

Because of this confidentiality, this type of factoring means a different process for collections. The company still sells the invoices to the factor, and the factor still pays cash for the invoices; however, the company maintains the sales ledger for the invoices and collects payments from its customers. The customer notifies the factor of all invoices sent and provides him with a monthly aging report on the outstanding invoices.

If the aging report is unfavorable, the factor has the right to increase retention or reserve with that company. The company is receiving its payments from the customers, but it must turn them over to the factor by depositing them into an account belonging to the factor. The factor can take over the arrangement and disclose itself to the customers if problems begin to arise with collections or in any other aspect. This type of factoring poses the greatest risk to the factor, and therefore is not used much in the industry.

If the customer is aware of the arrangement between the factor and the company, it is known as full-disclosure financing or a disclosed relationship. In this situation, the factor provides all the collection activity and manages the sales ledger for all of the company's factored invoices.

Roles in the Factoring Arena

In factoring, there are three roles available for someone wanting to work in this area. The first is to refer factoring deals to factors. The second is to broker factor transactions, and the third is to be a factor and invest in buying business invoices directly.

The first method of "referrals only" is the easiest way to get started in the industry. In referring business to factors, you would be responsible for finding good prospects, collecting basic information about the company and its invoices, and then providing this information to the factor. By doing this, you will receive a referral fee from the factor. After the referral is made, your responsibility with the transaction is over, and the factor handles the rest of the work.

A brokering arrangement is similar to the referral arrangement in that you are finding prospective companies for the factor. However, it differs in the amount of work you are responsible for. More of your time will be spent working with the companies and putting the deal together. This extra time and effort will net you a higher fee than the referral only. The remainder of this section will go into the brokering process in detail.

The last role you can choose to fill is that of being a factor yourself. This role carries the highest rewards, but also contains the most risk. Because you would actually be purchasing the company's invoices, you would be responsible for collections and the possibility of uncollectable accounts.

The Factoring Process

Let's now talk about the actual process that goes into factoring, and then give an example to clarify.

Step 1: Sales of Goods and Services —XYZ Company sells its widgets to its client, Smith Widgets.

Step 2: Invoicing —XYZ generates an invoice to Smith Widgets for thirty, sixty, or ninety days (depending on the relationship between XYZ and Smith)

Step 3: Decision to Factor —XYZ decides to factor its accounts receivable in order to generate some cash flow.

Step 4: Broker —XYZ meets with a broker to determine the best arrangement. If the broker is prepared to meet the needs of the company and deals professionally with the company, then XYZ moves forward with the deal.

Step 5: Paperwork —XYZ must assemble the paperwork necessary to document its customer base and start the factoring process. The broker may or may not help with this task. The broker is now the intermediary between XYZ and the factor who will be purchasing the invoices.

Step 6: Processing —After receiving the application package, the factor can then verify the details of the deal. The factor will determine the present value of the invoices, the rate of return, the discount to be applied, and their yield on investment.

Step 7: Agreement —Once the factor has decided to purchase the invoices of XYZ, he will create an accounts receivable purchase agreement. The agreement is made between XYZ and the factor.

Step 8: Notification —After the purchase agreement is signed, the factor then notifies XYZ's customers of the transaction and gets acknowledgement from each.

Step 9: Payment—The factor will pay XYZ for its invoices after receiving acknowledgment from XYZ's customers. Typically, a factor will pay the company based on the terms of the invoices. The shorter the terms on the invoice, the lower the factor's percentage of the total will be.

Here is a typical fee schedule based on the term of the invoice:

0-30 days	4%
31-60 days	8%
61-90 days	16%
Over 90 days	16-18%

The "count" begins on the day the factor pays the company, and ends when the factor is paid by the customer. A broker usually will earn 10-20% of the factor's fee, and is normally paid when the factor is paid.

Typically, a factor will pay the company in advance for the invoices based on some percentage, keeping a remainder in "reserve" for returns, damaged goods, etc. Once the factor is paid 100% of the invoices by the customer, the factor will remit the remainder of the invoices to the company, less his or her percentage. Let's take a look at an example.

XYZ sells $500 worth of widgets to Smith Widget. John Factor purchases that invoice from XYZ, paying 70% of the invoice ($350), twenty-four hours after the invoice is generated. Smith Widget pays John Factor $500 thirty days later. John Factor then pays XYZ the remainder of the Smith Widget's invoice less his 4% fee of $20, which comes out to $130. The $150 that was held in reserve can be tapped if Smith Widget doesn't pay the full amount of the invoice due to breakage, quality, or some other reason. In this case, John Factor would only repay XYZ the remainder less his fee and the amount withheld for damage.

Finding Factors and Clients

Factors

If you are looking to become a factoring broker, one of the first steps you will need to take is to develop a relationship with several factors. You don't want to work with just one, the reason being that different factors will have different criteria for the types of companies they will deal with. If you are working with only one, then you are locked into ONE type of factoring arrangement. Here are some questions you need to answer when working with or choosing a factor.

- What type of commission arrangement does the factor use? Determine how much your commission will be on referral. How and when will you be paid? You want to know if you will be paid forever on each payment received by the factor or if the commission will be effective for only a period of time?

- Does the factor work with independent brokers? You do not want to be locked into working with only one factor.

Make sure that the factor's agreement allows you to work with others.

- What kinds of written arrangements does the factor use? Will he or she be using a standard broker agreement or letter of agreement? You want your rights protected by some form of written agreement.

- What types of factoring do they offer? Does the factor offer recourse or non-recourse factoring? They may have different rates with the different risks involved.

Another thing to consider is the different services each factor offers. Large factoring companies will offer additional services to their client companies. These additional services can be filing and monitoring collections proceedings, handling routine collections of invoices, credit management, accounting services and more.

One of the things to remember when you are evaluating factors is that once you have entered into a professional arrangement with two or three factors, you must keep it professional. Do not plan to have a "stable" of factors and then "shop around" with your company to see which factor can give you the best deal. This is the fastest way to lose professional credibility. Most factors have very similar rates that the marketplace will bear. The reason to work with more than one factor is to provide your companies with a range of services, as well as meet the individual requirements of the factor. Fit the company with the factor that best meets its needs, not the one with the lowest price. That is a sure path to failure.

Potential Clients

To begin your search for potential factoring clients, you can look for new businesses, companies that have a problem with taxes or bankruptcy, and anyone you know that owns or works for a business. You can start by checking public records and local publications.

Business journals will list companies that have filed for Chapter 11 bankruptcy. Chapter 11 means that they are currently reorganizing their business but are still operating. Do not try to go to companies that have filed for Chapter 7 bankruptcy. This means they are going out of business. Because companies in Chapter 11 are reorganizing and trying to raise capital and save their company, they are terrific candidates for factoring because it quickly brings them the cash flow they desperately need.

Chapter 11 filing notices will give you a lot of information if you take the time. The notice will list the company's name, sometimes the name of the CEO, the address, and possibly any unsecured creditors. You can use this information in your marketing efforts to get a good idea of what a company does and who its suppliers are. These suppliers may also be potential clients for you because the company in Chapter 11 is not paying them. If that company is one of the supplier's major customers, that company may also be in trouble.

The same business journals list companies with tax problems. Look for a listing with the number 940 or 941. These numbers mean that the company has a payroll tax lien and have not paid all of their payroll taxes to the IRS yet. (A 1040 lien is a personal tax liability and not what you are looking for.) Again, this is another great possibility for a factoring client because of the need for quick cash. You will need to do good "follow up" on these types of prospects, however, because the information found in the journal may or may not be current. As a huge government entity, the wheels of the IRS grind slowly, and by the date of publication, the amount listed in the lien may have already been paid off. You will want to follow up with these companies to find out their current situation. The amount may have actually grown larger.

Use the Yellow Pages and just start sending out marketing literature and making calls to find "regular" companies that will benefit from factoring. Any product or service is a good candidate for factoring.

Using the Internet to search for companies in these fields can also help open up companies to your marketing efforts. Remember, your best bets are small to medium-sized companies that are growth oriented. These companies are usually on a tight budget and need capital so they can grow. The Internet can be a powerful sales tool if used creatively. And, unlike most reference sources, such as directories or almanacs, you can literally turn the Internet into whatever kind of sales resource you may need.

Remember, the Internet is an array of high- and poor-quality information. It's no longer enough to be "computer literate." Today, you must be "information literate" as well. Once you become familiar with the popular search engines, you'll find it easy to navigate this vast resource and its profusion of information. The ideal result: you'll be able to turn that information into knowledge, and that knowledge into prospects.

Research Your Prospects

Visit the Web sites of your prospects before making an in-person visit or initiating any communication like sending them letters or brochures. You'll gain insight into the prospect's corporate philosophy, culture, history, and management. If you are looking for a particular prospect's URL, or Web address, try www.(name of company).com. If this doesn't work, visit a search engine such as Yahoo or Google, and conduct a search on the name of the company. Also take the time to research your prospect's competitors. Each time you check out a prospect, visit the sites of its competitors. Learn about product and service differences between your prospect company and its competitors.

Direct Contact Sources

Accountants: one of the best sources of referrals. Accountants know when companies are experiencing financial difficulties with cash flow and can refer their clients to you for help in raising capital.

Tax Advisors: know when companies are having trouble paying their taxes. Can be another referral source for your services.

Financial Planners: similar to the two mentioned above, financial planners have the inside track on companies that need help.

Business Brokers: encounter possible factoring clients.

Commercial Insurance Agents: working with companies regularly, they can give you good ideas for types of companies to market to, as well as referrals of their own clients.

Government Purchasing Agents: these people are dealing every day with invoices and receivables. They are a good source for referrals.

Bankers: the commercial loan manager at a bank may be able to refer companies to you. Bankers have contact regularly with companies that are looking for financing but are unable to qualify. If the loan manager has your name as a reference, he or she is able to give these companies another option.

Business Consultants and Leaders: people in the industry who deal with their own companies and others. These are people who are great word-of-mouth sources for you. Make sure they have your card.

Making Presentations to Prospects

Let's discuss some general ideas that can help you when making presentations to your prospective clients. Remember that your presentation is an extension of yourself. If your prospect doesn't like you, he or she won't want to do business with you. Develop a rapport; be friendly. Don't be an overbearing or pushy salesperson. That turns people off and makes them want to leave. Even if your message is great, your attitude will push them away. Remember, this is a people-oriented business. Offer a solution to their problems.

Obviously, as we've mentioned before, be precise in obtaining the information required by the factor. Not having the proper information only slows the process down and ends up being a disservice to everyone involved, including yourself. Make sure that by the end of your presentation you have gone over the checklist that your factor requires so that you are ready to present it to your client as soon as the meeting is over. The last thing you want is to be called back because you've forgotten some small piece of information that the factor requires.

Ask your list of questions, but keep it conversational. You don't want to sound like an interrogator. If you can, try to gain the answers to your questions before you discuss your services. That way, you can better tailor your presentation or discussion to their particular needs. Write down any information that is important so that you don't forget it or let it fall through the cracks. Pay attention to the details, and it will reflect well on your professional credibility.

Going hand in hand with the details is educating your clients. Make sure that the companies you are dealing with understand the process. You want there to be no confusion about what factoring is and how the process works. Make sure they don't think it is a loan. Make certain they know how the process works and what their part in it will be. Ensuring that your customers are clear on this information will save a lot of headaches and confusion down the road.

Answering Objections

As you might expect, even while presenting the solutions to problems that prospective companies may have, you will still have objections. Here is a list of common responses you may run into, as well as ways to answer the issue. Later in this chapter, we will discuss advantages and costs, as well as ways to explain the costs to the client.

Only businesses that are failing use factoring. My company is not in trouble.

Assure the prospect that there are many successful and stable companies that take advantage of the services offered by factors. Give them a list of referral companies that they can contact and encourage them to contact those companies to get an idea of why and how they use factoring in their business.

Factoring is too expensive for our company.

Explain to the prospect again the variety of services provided and ask them to compare value. Remind them that paying their people to provide collection services costs them money, as does waiting for payment from their customers. Bank financing also costs money in the form of interest. (Look for more "answers" in the Advantages and Costs section in the following section.)

I won't know when my customers have paid and will lose touch with them.

Factors who manage accounts receivable for companies can provide more accurate and timely information than may have been possible from the prospect's own staff. This is largely due to the fact that factors are doing this business alone, whereas the A/R person on staff at a company may have many other tasks or jobs to fulfill.

I don't want to lose control of my business.

By outsourcing their receivables administration, the company actually gains greater control by freeing up money and resources to better manage its business, its customers, and its company direction and growth.

I don't want our financial statements to be negatively affected.

Factoring actually creates a positive influence on a company's financial statements because the payments for goods and services are received more quickly, goods and services are "turned over" more quickly, and cash is generated more quickly, creating an availability of funds.

Successful Presentation Hints

Following is a list of helpful hints that can aid you in creating and giving successful presentations. Keep them in mind before, during, and after your presentation.

Convenient Time: make sure that your meeting is scheduled at a time convenient for both of you. Take only the amount of time allotted; do not cause someone to fall behind in his or her schedule.

To the Point: during your presentation, get to the main point quickly and then back it up with facts.

Solve the Problem: plan and present your presentation in a way that shows a client how to solve its financial problems and meet its financial goals.

Attitude: be enthusiastic and professional.

Credibility: establish a rapport to build trust, confidence, and professional credibility.

Present Yourself: discuss your unique abilities to service the company's needs and solve their problems. Stress the advantages and value of your service.

Ask Questions: strive to ask intelligent questions and get a feel for the company's business practices and details. Ask for a tour of the company or a demonstration of their processes. Find out about how they work.

Discuss the Past: have they had bad experiences with factoring before? What have their experiences been with their financial situation in general?

Take Notes: make sure that you take detailed notes on every facet of the company's situation. Your notes will help you later on when presenting the company to the factor or when returning to follow up with the company.

Control: stay in control of the presentation. Make the prospect pay attention to you. Don't go overboard with materials that draw attention away.

Develop Relationship: try to develop a long-term relationship with the company. You want this company to do business with you and your factor for the long run. Focus on advantages besides just cash flow to show them the value in the long run.

Close the Deal: assume that you will close the deal. Keeping a positive mindset will help you to focus on closing the deal throughout your presentation.

Paperwork: review the information on the client inquiry form. Make the client qualify for your services. You want to do business with companies that will grow and prosper and allow you to do the same. Make sure you complete all the documents required by the factor. Double check so you don't have to scramble for that last form later on.

Advantages versus Costs

Many companies start to panic when they see the costs associated with factoring. Many even compare the short-term fee the factor charges (4%) with a long-term interest rate. This is like comparing apples to oranges, and we will talk about how to explain it more clearly. First, let's take an in-depth look at the advantages of factoring and working with a broker. By using these points in your marketing strategy, materials, and presentation, you can help your prospective clients to see how factoring can benefit them.

Increase in Capital

The company is able to create a stream of "instant" cash from selling their invoices, without losing control or giving up equity as collateral in traditional financing. Invoices are purchased immediately by the factor (usually within twenty-four to forty-eight hours), allowing the company to offer their clients terms without actually having to wait for the payments to be made. A company's accounts receivable is one of the company's biggest assets, and can be its best source of operating capital. By using their own assets to increase capital, many companies see factoring as a way to "work themselves out of trouble," and this appeals to many companies.

Factoring versus Financing

Factoring has many advantages when compared to traditional bank financing. It is much easier to deal with a factor than with a bank since factors are working with the companies face to face and make their own decisions. Traditional bank loans may require more time and much more stringent credit qualifications. A "real" person no longer makes loan decisions at bank; computers have completely taken this process over, using sophisticated financial software to determine whether to grant a loan.

Typically, start-up companies are the ones that need the most growth capital, but because of their lack of credit history, they cannot qualify for bank loans. However, many of the clients of these types of companies are established companies, making them excellent candidates for factoring. One of the great strengths of factors is their ability to recognize the businesses that are good/great candidates for factoring and then work with them where banks would not. Many companies complain that the only people who can qualify for a bank loan are those who don't need one.

Some of the qualifications that banks are looking for are consistent cash flow for at least three years, strong collateral, and the owner's personal financial commitment. For start-up companies, some or all of these things may be missing, making it impossible for them to qualify. In fact, even if an owner can commit personal assets to the company, his or her spouse's assets can be affected as well. It is a huge risk to take with your home and your personal possessions. In fact, a spouse's assets and even businesses can be seized as collateral if the company does not pay on its bank loans.

Factors have taken on the role that the banker did twenty or thirty years ago. You went to your local banker, who you perhaps knew, and sat down face to face to discuss a loan. Now, banks have strict guidelines and can't make decisions based on personal relationships. Factors have the ability to be flexible in this way. They can respond to the company's needs, providing as much or as little capital as needed. The company is dealing directly with the person who is providing the money. Factors are large enough to provide the funding you need, but small enough to give one-on-one access to the decision makers. A factor is not bogged down with committees and bureaucracy. This can definitely affect how quickly a company gets its funding, and, if they need to make payroll in seven days, it can be a big problem. Factoring approval typically take twenty-four hours with funding in seven to ten days. Banks can take thirty to sixty days just for approval, and then back on another thirty to forty-five days for funding.

Another advantage that factoring has over traditional financing is that factors typically do not have a maximum limit. They will buy as many invoices as you wish to factor. Banks will usually set a limit on how much you can borrow. Banks also have standard applications and loan documents for a company to fill out. These documents are based on the bank's needs. Factoring agreements are customized for each client, based on the client's needs.

Credit Rating

A company that does not have to incur more debt to stay in business will have a better credit rating than one that is mired in debt. Factoring provides financing that is not shown on the balance sheet, allowing the company to show a stronger cash position. The position of the business is not affected, keeping control and liquidity in the hands of the owners. When other financing methods are used, the company or bank providing the financing will place a lien against the company's assets as well as the personal assets of the owners. With factoring, no additional debt is incurred. Because of this, a company may be able to qualify for other financing, credit protection, and a better credit rating. In fact, factoring can increase a company's chances of restructuring the long-term debt they already have.

Cash on Hand

Many companies fail because they have underutilized their resources (specifically their A/R) and lost money that would have come to them had they been able to produce and sell more product.

Many businesses also receive terms from their suppliers. Factoring their own invoices can give a company the cash needed to qualify for discounts from their suppliers by paying cash up front. If a company's suppliers provide terms of 2/10, net 30 (a 2% discount for payment within ten days, or full payment in thirty days), a company can offset much or all of the cost of factoring by paying these invoices immediately.

A company can also take advantage of gaining better relationships with its suppliers and vendors. The quick-paying customers of these suppliers are the ones who will be treated the best. By becoming a quick-paying customer, a company can begin to negotiate even more favorable terms. Some companies can even negotiate cash on delivery (or COD) terms with their suppliers with discounts of up to 4-5%. This would most likely offset the entire cost of the factor's fee.

Once a company has the capital to buy more supplies, they then have the ability to make and sell more products, generating more invoices. This all adds up to more cash directly to the bottom line of the company.

By receiving this infusion of cash from factoring, a company can also pay bills, clear up other debt and obligations, and basically get itself "together" financially. By "cleaning up its financial act," a company can improve its financial position. Many companies move from factoring to traditional financing once their positions have improved to the point where banks and other sources look upon them favorably.

No Long-Term Contract

A company can choose to sell one batch of invoices to a factor or establish an ongoing relationship. There are no long-term contracts that they must lock themselves into. The company can also determine which accounts to factor and hold onto any they wish to.

Save on Collection Costs

Companies must spend money collecting from clients who are not making their payments. Credit investigations, slow playing customers, bad debts, monthly statements, and collection calls all cost the company time and money. Factoring turns all of these responsibilities over to the factor, freeing up even more money for the company. Allowing the factor to perform these duties leads to greater efficiency for the company's employees to handle other tasks devoted to sales and profits.

Customer Relations

Because the factor is the one handling credit checks and managing the collections, the company can become "detached" from this part of the process, maintaining a better "image" and relationship with its clients. The factor can now play the "bad guy," while the company remains out of the "fight," so to speak. When the factor becomes the person checking the credit of the customers, the company will also benefit from the factor's impartiality. Consider this example— when a salesperson is trying to close a large deal or account, he or she may overlook certain red flags associated with credit difficulties. He may even walk the deal through existing controls in the company in order to "force" it through the system. This may close the deal, but if the customer can't pay, it does the company more harm than good. A factor will not be affected by the desire to close a deal and will conduct a thorough credit check on that customer, possibly protecting the company from a bad deal.

Even if the factor does not decide to buy the invoices of a customer with questionable credit, the company still has the flexibility to continue to sell to that customer and carry the invoice itself. Factoring does not mean that a company has to tighten its credit restrictions so much that it has no customers left. The factor is simply protecting himself against those who may be credit risks. A factor will also routinely check the credit of a company's ongoing customers to ensure that the customer continues to be good credit risk. Most companies do not do this, and having the factor perform this function will aid the company even more by warning them of potential hazards that lay ahead with their current customers.

The factor is also responsible for obtaining an acknowledgement from each of the company's customers for each invoice that is owed.

By doing this, the factor can quickly and easily ensure that the invoice will be paid. However, there is a side benefit to this process. By requiring the customer to acknowledge the shipment, the factor has a build-in method of ensuring that the order is correct and the customer is satisfied with the shipment. If not, the company can immediately turn around and remedy the situation. By this method, the company is able to keep fantastic customer relations because of its quick handling of whatever the issue may be.

In this situation, the company is also protected from its customers returning unsold merchandise at a later date claiming it was damaged or otherwise unsellable. In many cases, unethical companies will do this to avoid having to "eat" merchandise they purchased but cannot sell. By having an acknowledgement from the customer up front, the factor protects the company from this practice. The acknowledgment states that the customer intends to pay and that the shipment is satisfactory. After signing this form, a customer cannot later claim the shipment was damaged or unsellable and demand a costly return.

Real Costs of Factoring

Earlier, we talked about the fees involved with the purchase of business invoices, and many companies see 4% (or more) of an invoice as too high to pay. Let's take a minute to take a good look at the costs versus benefits of factoring.

Almost all companies extend terms of thirty to ninety days to their customers. In this situation, they are granting an interest-free loan for that amount of time to their customers. If these customers went to a bank to borrow the amount of money they owe Company ABC in invoices, the bank would certainly charge them interest.

Now, take Company ABC. They are currently granting interest-free loans to their customers, and then they are missing out on opportunities to make money they would have had if their customers had paid sooner. Let's look at how they are missing out.

ABC has an average of $500,000 in receivables at any give time. Most of their customers pay within thirty to forty-five days, and some spread it out to sixty days. The company is financially stable, but consistently has $150,000 in back orders. They do not have the cash to purchase the materials or pay the labor to fill these back orders.

Now, let's look at the cost of interest-free financing ABC is offering. Annual interest at 12% on $500,000 for thirty days is $5,000 ($500,000 A/R x 12% = $60,000 divided by 12 months = $5,000 a month). That means that over a year, ABC is losing $60,000 to the "interest-free financing" it is granting its customers! This is interest that never gets charged or collected—it is lost.

On top of lost "interest," consider opportunity cost. About 15-20% of purchase orders that become back ordered by a company get cancelled because the customer simply decides not to wait and takes his or her business elsewhere. That means that ABC is losing 20% of $150,000 in orders every month because they cannot keep up on their back orders. That is $30,000 a month or $360,000 a year.

Additionally, if those back orders were produced during the same month, the profit on those orders, after subtracting the cost of goods sold and labor, would go directly to the bottom lone, increasing the profitably of the company. This is the missed opportunity, and all because the company is forced to wait for customers to pay.

So, what is the cost of 4% factoring fee to a company? Help your potential clients to see the big picture. As we discussed in the section on advantages, simply taking advantage of or negotiating cash discounts can completely or partially offset the factor's fee. Here is a concrete example that will help them to understand.

SmithCo has gross revenues of $100,000 per month without factoring. The cost of goods sold is 65%, which results in gross profits of $35,000. Overhead is $32,000, which leaves a net profit of $3,000.

Now consider what additional cash flow would enable them to do, such as take discounts for volume purchases, increase sales and advertising efforts, or add a second shift. By factoring the first $100,000, we can project a doubling of revenue to $200,000 with a consistent 65% of cost of goods sold (though this cost may actually decrease if they can negotiate discounts for paying cash). This puts the gross profit at $70,000. Subtract overhead of $44,000 (which is more, but never double) and the cost of factoring which is $6,000, and SmithCo has realized a net profit of $20,000.

In this instance, which is typical, the decision NOT to factor would have cost SmithCo $20,000 in missed opportunity for one month.

How Expensive is Factoring?

Once you have the client figure out how much it costs them to pay their staff to send out invoices, deposit checks, log payments, produce reports, and handle collections, they can see that factoring can indeed provide more benefits than costs. Tell them to ask themselves two questions:

1. Will the cash advanced allow me to make more money (one way or another) than the fees charged?

2. Will factoring allow me to stay in business?

By evaluating and weighing the costs versus benefits, a company should be able to make an informed decision about whether factoring is right for them.

A quick note to you, as a broker. If the company is going to use the proceeds of factoring to do more business and increase their production capability, then they are probably stable, good prospects. If they plan to use the money to pay overhead, clean up bad debts, pay past invoices, then they may be too far in the hole to be saved. The chart below compares factoring to other options that a company might have in raising capital. One can clearly see that in most cases factoring is usually a great option for a company to consider.

	Factoring	Leasing	Going Public	Venture Capital	Bank Loan	Private Investors	Govt. Programs
Simple application	Yes	No	No	No	No	Varies	No
Personal guarantees	No	Maybe	No	No	Yes	No	Maybe
Days to fund	3-10	15-30	120-270	90-180	60-180	15-90	60-180
Approval based on credit	No	Yes	Yes	Yes	Yes	Yes	Yes
Funding tied to sales	Yes	No	No	No	No	No	No
Give up equity	No	No	Yes	Yes	No	Yes	No
Give up control	No	No	Maybe	Yes	No	Maybe	Maybe
Limited to asset value	No	Yes	No	No	Yes	Maybe	Yes
Require profitability	No	Usually	Yes	Usually	Yes	Usually	Usually
Ongoing monitoring	No	No	Yes	Yes	Yes	Yes	Yes
Reduce overhead	Yes	No	No	No	No	No	No

Qualifying Clients

When evaluating prospective clients, you must know the

qualifications that a company must meet in order to be considered by a factor. These qualifications will vary among different factors, but most will want the following information:

- Type of business
- How the company conducts its affairs
- Characteristics of its customers
- Annual business revenue of $500,000 or more

This last qualification is not set in stone, as many factors are willing to work with companies with much lower annual revenues. Most factors tend to focus on small to medium-sized companies as their clients. Here are some characteristics that tend to make a good potential candidate.

- Newly established
- Growth oriented
- Lack adequate financing
- Difficulty meeting operating expenses
- May have tax problems or bankruptcy potential
- Little or no net worth

Companies in these situations make good potential clients for factors because they are motivated to receive the increased cash flow from selling their invoices. Companies that are willing to sell their receivables can be found in just about every industry that supplies products or services to other businesses. More and more companies are dealing on an international level, as well as outsourcing many of their services such as janitorial and human resources. Because of this, you have an enlarged arena of service outsourcing companies that you can approach with a factoring opportunity.

The growing trend toward international trade is also expanding the number of companies that are willing to factor their business invoices. Because companies are now being required to extend terms to international customers, the time and money involved in establishing credit worthiness and collecting from foreign customers increases. Factors willing to tap into this growing market can find themselves truly successful as domestic companies scramble to get rid of dealing with collecting from their international customers. Many factors have even joined forces with others around the world to create branches in various countries and areas to handle the growing demand for international factoring.

Gathering Information

The broker is responsible for gathering preliminary information on potential clients to present to the factor. Here is some of the information that a typical factor would want:

- Company Name (or DBA) and Address
- Phone and Fax Number
- Contact Person's Name
- Type of Business
- How Long in Business
- Date of Incorporation
- Monthly Sales and Percentage to Factor
- Average Dollar Amount of Invoices
- Payment Terms
- Accounts Receivable Pledged as Collateral for Other Loans
- Outstanding Bank Loans or Lines of Credit and Collateral Used to Secure
- Type and Business Nature of Customers
- List of Regular Customers and Each Customer's Monthly Sales Volume

Once you have found a prospective client and gathered this information, it is time to present the candidate to the factor. If the factor is satisfied with the information that you have provided, he or she will then contact the prospective client to begin the application process. You should remain involved at this point so that you can help your prospective company with the application forms and information. Here is some of the information that will be included/ required in a typical application package:

- Application form: details about the company, owners, and officers.

- Purchase and sale agreement: a legal form that transfers ownership of the accounts receivable from the company to the factor.

- List of company's customers: a list and credit rating on each of the company's customers.

- Acknowledgement and representation form: a document that states that any payments received by the company from its customers for invoices owned by the factor will be forwarded to the factor.

- Certificate of corporate resolution: if the client company is a corporation, this form identifies the officers of the corporation and indicates their agreement to the factoring relationship.

- Accounts receivable aging schedule: this shows how long it takes each of the company's customers to pay.

- Articles of incorporation and corporate charter (of a corporation).

- Partnership agreement (if a partnership).

- Bulk assignments schedule: this lists the invoices/receivables that the company is selling to the factor and lists the details of each customer.

- UCC-1 form: used to record the factor's lien on the company's accounts receivable asset. Once the invoices are sold to the factor, this form must be filled out and filed with the secretary of state, the county clerk's office, or both. This is an important form for the factor, and must not be overlooked.

- Acknowledgment form: used to inform the company's customers of the new arrangement and provide new payment information directing payments to the factor. A form is completed and sent to each customer listed on the bulk assignment schedule once the invoices are sold. The customer must sign and return the form indicating that the product or service was received and accepted.

Some of these forms may not be included in the initial application package. The last three, which deal with the actual purchase and assignment of the invoices, may be dealt with later in the process.

Once the company has prepared the application package, the factor will evaluate the company by reviewing their records and operational performance. Some of the records and information that the factor will evaluate are financial statements, tax records, and accounts payable aging statements. The reason for this is that a factor wants to ensure that he or she is buying the invoices of a stable company that will not be going out of business or in some way "short changing" its customers. By evaluating these documents, the factor can see if the business meets its payroll and pays its bills and taxes.

Another evaluation would be to see if there are any liens against the company by checking states and county UCC records. By looking into state and local UCC records, the factor can get better insight into the company's past business practices.

Next, the factor would analyze the company's customers by checking their credit ratings and payment history. Since the customers are the ones actually paying the factor this evaluation must be conducted to ensure that the invoices will, indeed, be paid. By scrupulously checking the credit rating and status of both the company and its customers, the factor can better control his risk before he agrees to purchase any of the company's invoices.

After the application and evaluation process is complete, the factor will then agree to purchase the company's invoices. If the evaluation was unfavorable, the factor would then close the deal without the purchase decision. When the factor does agree to purchase the accounts receivable, the company will usually receive 70-80% of the face value of the invoice (the advance) from the factor. The remaining percentage (the reserve), less the factor's fee, will be paid to the company once the factor receives payment from the customer.

Factoring Consideration

The client company and the factor need to be aware of a few considerations. By familiarizing yourself with these issues, you can better answer questions and give information to your client companies that is more detailed and clear.

Rebates

If a customer pays early, the company does not usually get any rebate from the factor.

Buy-backs

In a non-recourse agreement, the only time a factor can "return" the invoice to the client company is when there is fraud, or a problem with the merchandise or service. A factor does not have to keep an invoice where the company has sold substandard merchandise that the customer will not accept. In any other case, the factor has the sole responsibility of collecting from the non-paying customer.

Credit Limits

The factor has the right to set a credit limit for each of a client's customers. If credit limits are set, the client company cannot extend credit for a particular customer past his or her individual limit. This will help the factor minimize the risk of getting too far in "the hole" with a customer, and stops the problem at a certain level if the customer stops paying.

Invoices to Factor

A company may sell any particular account to a factor and determine which ones to hold back. However, once a company has sold a particular account, all invoices for that account must be offered to the factor in the future.

Invoices to Purchase

A factor is not required to purchase any account from the company, and may "pick and choose" which accounts to purchase. The factor may even select any number of invoices from a particular account without purchasing all of the invoices in that account. The factor can refuse to purchase any invoice that is offered.

Non-Payment

If a customer cannot pay, the factor cannot receive money from future payments that the company receives. The only recourse a factor has is to collect from the customer on the invoice he has purchased. The factor CAN get payment from the company if there is a problem with the shipment or service. Now, let's look at an example of a factoring deal brokered by you from start to finish.

Through one of your marketing sources, you have found a potential company that we will call Trinity Inc. You spend some time on the phone with them, and determine that they would be a good possibility for one of your factors.

At this point, you begin collecting information on Trinity, using the forms required by that particular factor. After looking at the preliminary data, the factor sends you an application package for Trinity to fill out. You, as the broker, will work with the people at Trinity to prepare all of the paperwork necessary to complete the application process, and then submit it back to the factor for review.

After evaluating the application package, the factor decides to accept Trinity as a new client. At this point, the broker's task is done. However, let's continue the process to see how the process works being the factor.

Trinity Inc. decides that it will factor most of its invoices, but it already has preprinted invoice stock. Your factor provides them with a stamp that they can use on their invoices that states that the invoice has been assigned. This way, Trinity can notify customers of where payment should be sent, without having to change their invoice stock.

Now that Trinity is an existing client of your factor, each time they want to assign a new invoice, they simply generate the invoice, stamp it, and send it to the customer. Trinity must complete a bulk assignment schedule of the invoices they wish to sell, and submit it to the factor. They must also include copies of the invoices.

When the factor receives the bulk assignment schedule and invoice copies, he or she will generate an acknowledgment form for all customers listed on the schedule, informing them of the payment situation. The form will let each customer know that the invoice has been assigned, and to make payment directly to the factor instead of to Trinity Inc. Each customer should check the invoice information on the form, sign it, and return it to the factor.

Once the factor receives the forms back from Trinity's customers, he or she will then pay Trinity 70% (or the agreed upon percentage) of the invoice totals. Depending on how quickly Trinity's customers pay, the factor will deduct his or her fee and remit the remaining balance once each invoice is paid.

Chapter 7

Investing in Other Debt Instruments

As we have seen with the other chapters in this book, cash flow investing is all about finding the right situations where people want or need cash for their assets, and then purchasing them at a discount in order to generate a profit or positive cash flow.

This chapter deals with purchasing debt instruments (other than notes and mortgages). There are many different opportunities for cash flow investing. In fact, anytime there is a "promise" to pay over a period of time, you can offer to buy this "income stream" for cash now. Some types of income streams that we will cover are:

- Promissory Notes
- Inheritance
- Property Lease
- Lottery Winnings

Since debt instruments comprise a very broad area, it is best to choose a different area of cash flow investing for your main business, and then, once you are familiar with the industry, bring in debt instrument investing as a niche that fits with your primary strategy.

This market is relatively new and thus wide open for cash flow investors. By positioning yourself between the party who is making the payments and the person receiving them, you can create a winning situation for both.

Basics of the Debt Instrument Arena

Just like a note, any income stream is an asset that can be bought and sold. The person who is owed the income can sell his or her right to receive the income in return for receiving immediate cash. Just as in the note arena, some people no longer can or want to receive a monthly payment on a total. They would rather take a slightly discounted amount of the total in order to have the cash immediately. In this arena, you can fulfill three roles: referral, broker, and funding source.

Referral

If you want to simply collect a referral fee, this is the way to go. This role involves funding debt instruments for sale and referring them to a broker or investor. You would also collect some basic information from the seller to provide to the funding source, but after that, your responsibilities would end. You would receive a referral fee and the investor would handle the rest.

Broker

A broker's work is similar to that of a simple referral with one exception—after you have found a seller, you would work with both the seller and the investor to put the deal together. Negotiating with both sides would be required, as well as any paperwork that needs to be handled. Because of the extra effort, the fees a broker receives are much grater than fees received from referrals only.

Funding Source

Investing in debt instruments can be a risky but very profitable role. Debt instruments are very high-yield investments, and if you are looking for a profitable place to invest funds, it can be a huge moneymaker for you.

Debt Instrument Transactions

Because of the nature of the variety of debt instruments that exist, each transaction will be different based on the debt that is involved. However, there are some basic steps that are common to all debt instrument transactions.

- Locate a seller

- Gather personal and financial information regarding seller and debt instrument

- Determine whether the debt instrument is assignable

- Present information to funding source

- Practice due diligence

- Present offer to seller

- Fill out contract or purchase agreement

- Closing (transfer of ownership documents, etc.)

- Payment

These are the steps that are common to any debt instrument deal. There may be other steps, legal or otherwise, that may be required for any particular type of debt instrument.

Types of Debt Instrument

Automobile

When people finance car purchases, they agree to pay monthly to the holder of the note. Many small car dealerships provide their own financing. Because they are not large national dealerships, they may not wish to hold these notes for the term (two to four years), and would rather sell the note in exchange for cash now. They may need it to buy new inventory, pay operating expenses, payroll, etc. In finding and working with automobile notes, the following information is needed:

- Business information of seller
- Corporate name and phone
- DBA name
- Mailing address
- Physical address

- Landlord or mortgage company name and phone
- Any additional locations—do they have other dealerships?
- Owners—name, SSN, birth date, title, percent of ownership, address
- Previous experience—experience level of owners
- Key personnel—employees of dealership
- Information on notes being sold
- Name and address of payer
- Year, make, and model of vehicle
- Odometer reading when sold
- VIN
- Monthly payment on note
- Term of note
- Current balance
- Interest rate

Once you have presented this information to the funding source, that person will perform his or her due diligence. In this case, the person will need to check the risk of each payer.

As in factoring, automobile notes can be bought "recourse" or "non-recourse." In a recourse deal, the dealership still holds the risk of non-payment. In non-recourse, the funding source assumes the risk.

After the deal is completed, the funding source will ensure that his or her name becomes the primary lien holder on the vehicle to provide collateral in case of non-payment.

Business Notes

When someone wants to sell his or her business, it is similar to selling a home or other asset. However, it is difficult for buyers of businesses to qualify for traditional financing, so the seller may be forced to provide financing for the purchase of the business. This is almost exactly the same as seller financing in Real Estate notes, except that furniture, fixtures, equipment, and receivables that are owned by the business, instead of a home, secure the note. Inventory can also be used to secure notes.

The steps to go about handling a business note are the same as a real estate note. Gather the information required by the funding source and present the deal. The funding source will evaluate the deal and offer a quote. After the funding source has performed his or her due diligence, he or she will make an offer, close the deal, and fund the deal.

Purchase Orders and Contracts

When a company issues a purchase order, it is basically giving a promise to buy a certain product or service at a specific price. Although not technically a debt instrument, purchase orders and contracts can still be bought by cash flow investors because they are promises to pay. The main reason a company may sell its purchase orders or contracts is that it may need the capital that will be paid by those contracts to purchase the materials to fulfill the contracts. This is basically advance funding, and it is usually generated by factoring activities.

Like factoring account receivables, advance funding of purchase orders and contracts can give a company money needed for cost of production, freight insurance, duties, and other costs involved in filling the order. It can also give a company the opportunity to take advantage of supplier discounts for paying in cash up front.

Commercial and Property Leases

A commercial lease is a contract signed between the owner of a commercial property and the tenant who operates a business in the building. The lease can have a term as short as a few months to as long as several years. A lease can be compared to a renter who rents an apartment in which to live. A lease is simply a business that is "renting" office space.

Because a lease payment is a stream of income for the owner of the building, it becomes a cash flow investment opportunity. By selling the lease for cash (at a discount) now, the property owner receives the cash in exchange for the future income of the lease.

Tax Certificates

Tax certificates are relatively unheard of, but are high-yield/low-risk investments that can work for you or your investors. The processes involved are:

- A property owner cannot pay his or her property tax.

- The government places the property into tax default.

- The government (desiring cash now) issues tax certificates than can be purchased by investors for the amount of the tax owed plus interest, fees, etc.

- Within a specified amount of time, the homeowner must pay the tax or face foreclosure.

- The investor can redeem the certificate after a period of time and receive the return on his or her investment.

Most states sell the tax certificates at public auction where investors can bid against one another to purchase the certificates. By buying at auction, investors hope to increase their return on investment by getting a "bargain." However, bidding against others can defeat that purpose. You can also purchase them over the counter at the county office.

Tax certificates have been a well-kept secret in the past, but they are an excellent investment because they offer guaranteed higher yields than traditional investments (401k, certificates of deposits, etc.). The investor never has to deal with the homeowner; the county still assumes the responsibility of collecting the taxes owed. After a certificate is issued, the homeowner has an amount of time, called the redemption period, in which to pay the back taxes. If the homeowner does not pay within this time, his or her home will be foreclosed on. After the redemption period, the investor returns to the county office, signs over the certificate, and receives a check.

The reasons why tax certificates are such good investments are the yield and the redemption period. A typical CD may yield 4% annual interest on your investment; whereas tax certificates can yield anywhere from 15% to 24%, depending on the state. Some of the states that have the highest yields are: Michigan, Indiana, Wyoming, Arizona, Massachusetts, Maryland, New Jersey, Florida, New Hampshire, Illinois, and Iowa.

The redemption period on a tax certificate can vary from state to state as well. Many states have a two-year redemption period while others may give the homeowner anywhere from five to seven years to pay the delinquent tax.

To find tax certificates to purchase, do your research at the county tax collector's office. Make sure the property that is the collateral on the certificate is evaluated, since this is what protects your investment.

Marine and Aerospace Notes

Like automobile loans, when people buy and sell boats or airplanes, they also need financing to pay for it. Sometimes the seller of a boat or plane must offer financing to the buyer, if the buyer cannot qualify for other financing. Cash flow investors can purchase marine and aerospace notes from either the seller, if it was seller financed, or from a dealer.

As with other debt instruments, you will need to gather all the information on the buyer and seller, as well as the plane or boat, and present it to the funding source. Follow the same general steps with these types of notes as you would with automobile and other notes.

Equipment Notes and Leases

When a company needs to buy expensive equipment, many times it will lease rather than pay the entire cost up front. There are two types of equipment leases:

True Lease

This does not create a security interest when the cost of the lease is much higher than the cost of the equipment. The company leasing the equipment assumes the risk of loss and agrees to pay taxes, insurance, recording, and service costs.

Finance Lease

This is an arrangement where a leasing company works with the equipment supplier to pay for the equipment after it has been delivered to the company leasing it.

Many companies today lease their equipment, and many times, it is huge, expensive machinery or vehicles that take years to pay off. The companies that are providing the leases to these companies often need to sell the leases to obtain cash now.

Mobile Home Notes

Like many other seller-financed assets, mobile homes are another area where sellers may hold the notes on the sale of the home. There are also a small number of mobile home dealers who may finance the sale of a mobile home. By identifying clients in these two areas, you can easily make the purchase of mobile home notes part of your cash flow investment strategy.

There are a few things to consider when purchasing mobile home notes. If the home is truly mobile, then it can be treated in the same manner as automobile note, with the same procedures and documents. If the home is attached to property, then the procedures and documents will be more like a real estate note.

Many mobile homes are located in a mobile home park. They have had the wheels removed and are placed on concrete foundations. This is known as being pit set. Because it costs from $3,000-$5,000 to move a mobile home that has been pit set, these types of homes are considered more secure, with less investment risk.

Lottery Winnings

In most states, when people win the lottery jackpot, they receive their winnings in annual payments over a twenty-year period. Very few states even offer the winner the option to take the money in one lump sum. The reasoning behind this is that the winners are protected from squandering their newfound wealth all at once. However, many winners would rather have their winnings in one lump sum so that they can invest, buy a home, pay off debts, or send a child to college.

Cash flow investors can also buy lottery winnings from the winners, paying them a discounted cash amount now for the future stream of income. An investor then receives the payments directly from the lottery commission, and a lottery winner must declare the lump sum payment as taxable income.

To combat this tax concern, the funding source can make a loan against the future annual payments. This loan is structured as if the lottery winner received the annual check, less tax withholding, and endorsed it over to the funding source for loan repayment each year. The up-front lump sum will be less when using this method, but the proceeds will not be considered taxable income. The interest on the "loan" can even be tax deductible (depending on the use of the proceeds).

Structured Settlements and Annuities

A structured settlement is a stream of income paid to someone as a result of some sort of lawsuit, usually personal injury. The income is funded through an annuity purchased from a major life insurance company or Treasury bond trusts.

An annuity is a contract sold by an insurance company that guarantees payment to the holder at a future date, usually retirement.

As with any future stream of income, those people who are receiving settlement payments monthly are potential clients of cash flow investors if they would rather receive a lump sum payment now rather than continue to receive the monthly payment. Documents that are need for such a transaction are:

- Certified copy of the case settlement: this tells what the case was about, and how and when the court settled the case.

- Annuity: this indicates who is responsible for paying the settlement, usually an insurance company. It also lists who is receiving the payments and the payment terms.

- Opinion Letter: before the deal can be finalized, the seller's attorney must write a letter stating that the seller was counseled on all of the ramifications of selling his or her settlement and that he or she understands the details of the deal or transaction.

Workers' compensation is a type of structured settlement, but it is very complicated with legal concerns. If you find a client who wants to sell a workers' compensation settlement, direct the person to the funding source and let the investor handle the rest. You will be paid a commission for the referral.

Viatical Settlements

A viatical settlement is the sale of a person's life insurance policy at a discount of face value for immediate cash. Viatical settlements are an excellent way to give options to people who are facing a terminal or life-threatening illness. Many people do not realize that they can utilize their life insurance while they are still alive, instead of allowing their life insurance to lapse. Viatical settlements eliminate the risk of a lapsed policy because the viatical settlement company takes over responsibility for the premiums.

By purchasing the future stream of income for immediate cash, cash flow investors and viatical settlement companies allow the terminally ill patient to determine how to allocate this valuable asset.

As long as the person's insurance policy has been in effect for more than the contestable period (usually two years), he or she may be eligible. As long as the ownership of the policy is transferable, almost any kind of life insurance policy can be viaticated.

The viatical settlement company will review the information you have gathered and then make an evaluation of the person's medical condition and the insurance policy. The amount of the policy paid in cash is typically from 40-85% of the face value, and is usually paid within three to five weeks of application, depending on how long it takes to obtain medical records and other information.

Inheritance

People have the ability to take advances on their inheritances. It's a common practice, and trust beneficiaries can receive immediate cash in exchange for a future distribution from a probate or trust.

The process of investing by purchasing inheritance distributions is complex. As a broker, you should expect to fill the role of making referrals to the investor and gathering the basic information. The funding source will generally have his or her own legal staff and will handle the rest of the deal.

Ways to find potential clients:

- Research court records

- Search public probate records

- Direct contact sources — attorneys and financial planners

As we've seen in this chapter, there are many other avenues that can be tapped once you have determined the area of cash flow investing you would like to work. Many of the areas we have discussed in this chapter can be merged nicely into your main business as a secondary source of clientele and revenue.

Chapter 8

Negotiation

A key part of cash flow investing is how to negotiate a deal. Always remember that the seller is motivated to sell and that you do NOT have to buy. You want to be willing and able to walk away from the deal if the seller will not accept the offer you make. Do not get so wrapped up in closing the deal that you bargain away your profit margin! Know the maximum price you are willing to pay on a deal and don't exceed it. If the seller is desperate enough, he or she will be willing to come down to your offering price.

Another area where you will have to negotiate is when dealing with partners or buyers/renters. In this case, you need to be firm with your position without offending or angering the people you are working with. When negotiating with potential buyers or renters, you need to ensure that they understand ALL of your conditions. Make it plain to them what your responsibilities are and what their part is in the transaction. Decide how you want your financing to be structured and don't waver from that stance. You may make allowances in other areas in order to help them to feel like they are getting a good deal, but stand firm on your financing.

When dealing with business partners, whether the funding source or a repair person, try to create a win-win situation that doesn't cost you more money than you are willing to give away.

In the cash flow investing world, everything is built on relationships. Every contact you make is important because you never know when someone you meet could be a future buyer, seller, or investor. However, before someone will work with you, you must establish a relationship of trust.

The Art of Negotiation

The art of negotiation is one that you can learn and master with practice. You need to have the right attitude, ask the right questions, and listen. By doing this, you can instill a feeling of trust and confidence in the person with whom you are negotiating. There are some basic steps to follow when you are negotiating, and we will take the time to go over them so you can begin to master the art of negotiation.

Shower the Client with Attention

Everyone likes to be the center of attention. You need to make your clients feel important and give them all your undivided attention. Treat them with respect. Don't take cell phone calls during your meeting with them. Don't zone out when they are talking about unimportant things. Make sure they know you are listening to them by using your body language to develop rapport, and by restating their comments to ensure you are clear on everything they are saying.

Find out About the Client

Get to really know your clients. People like to talk about themselves, and the more you know them personally, the more they are likely to trust you professionally. Also, in the process of getting to know them, you will understand their needs a lot better. This in turn may help you find better deals for them or turn them into future money partners or buyers.

Relax

The atmosphere when meeting with clients needs to be relaxed and comfortable. Use a relaxed style of conversation. Don't overwhelm clients with big words or concepts they might not understand. Have fun and enjoy what you are doing. It will come through in your tone of voice and actions. Stay professional, but not stuffy.

Find Something in Common

By finding a common ground with the client, you can begin to build rapport with them. Listen and observe when they talk or when you visit them at home. When you have found a hobby or interest in common, you've just broken down one barrier between you and the client. Having something to discuss other than work will help them feel more comfortable.

Be a Problem Solver

In being helpful to your clients, sometimes you will need to come up with creative ideas to solve problems. Be flexible and think about the options that will best suit everyone. By doing this, it will help reinforce the trust you have developed with clients, and help them to realize that you are doing everything you can to create the best deal. Come up with several options to solve their problems. Use combinations of financing to create the most profitable deals for all parties involved.

Be an Effective Listener

This key "rule" underpins the other things we've talked about. Effective listening will help in all of the areas we've discussed. Even if you think you are a good listener, you can still get better. Listening is not the same as hearing. You need to listen with your brain, not just your ears. Listen to what clients want. Restate their key points back to them to show that you understand all of their specific needs.

Control the Conversation

Focus on the clients' needs and ask the right questions. This will help you stay in control of the situation. Remember that, in the end, you are in the business of making a profit. Once you lose control of a negotiation, your profits can begin to head downward.

Wait to Make an Offer

Don't make an offer in the initial conversation, especially over the telephone. Wait to make an offer until you have met with the client to find out what he or she really needs and wants from the deal. By making an offer too quickly, you can miss out on other opportunities to make a profit.

Don't Push

Don't act like a pushy salesperson. Overbearing salespeople have given a bad reputation to everyone in sales over the years. Clients are naturally wary of someone acting too pushy to sell them on something. Keep clients at ease, and keep situations comfortable. You don't want to get your clients' defenses up. Earn their trust and gain their cooperation. By doing these "basics," you can develop relationships with your clients and put them at ease. You will be better able to gain their trust, which can make it easier to close the deal. Let's now look at some negotiation strategies that you can use to help grow your business.

Initial Meeting

Be Professional

Use the first meeting with the client to establish a professional image. Then, as you meet with them further, you can develop rapport, raise the comfort level, and make the situation more casual.

Make an Appointment

Set an time to meet with clients and be on time. Ask them to prepare the documents ahead of time that you will need at the meeting. Provide them with your initial questions so that they are ready to respond with accurate, "realistic" answers.

Meet with the Decision Maker

If the husband is the key decision maker, it will do you no good to meet with the wife alone. It will only guarantee that she will say, "I have to talk to my husband about this." The same goes for business partners. Make sure that you have everyone who will have a say in the decision involved in the meeting. In these cases, you will have to build a relationship with each one.

Take it Slow

In the first meeting, you don't want to launch into a sales

presentation. You want to take the time to get to know your clients. You need to develop a relationship of trust with them. If you show up with your "selling points," they will only see a salesperson, not a partner. Find out what their needs are first. It will help you tailor the deal to best meet their particular situation.

Determine Specifics

After you have gained their trust, have them tell you the specifics about the deal and what they want to gain. Develop a team approach to solving their problem. Ask them their opinion, and make suggestions. Give options, and see how they react to certain scenarios. Many people have never heard of the types of financing that you may propose. It may be something they never thought of, but will be perfect for their situation.

Don't Rush

Do not appear to need the deal, no matter how badly you may need to close. Once the client knows that you are desperate, the balance of power will have shifted to their side. You in turn will become the motivated party and lose the chance of making a profit.

How Much and Why

Find out why the client is selling and how much the client needs from the deal. This will help you to better understand his or her motivation in selling. Some clients might have medical bills they need to pay, while others might need to pay off their mortgage that they are three months behind on. Ask them what they would like to see happen as a result of selling. Ask the client to suggest a fair price. Finding out these things will help you to tailor the best financial package for them and will help you to set the parameters of your offer.

Promise to Return with Options

Let your clients know at the end of the meeting that you will take the time to explore all avenues available and will come up with some options that will suit their needs. Always show a sense of urgency since the less motivated clients will sometimes change their minds as time passes.

Follow-Up Meeting

Present the Options

At the next meeting with the clients, present all of the options you have prepared. Do not bring only one offer. Play with the numbers ahead of time and determine several different avenues you could take. Make sure all of the options meet their needs. You want them to be able to choose.

Make the Offer

Make your offer to your clients based on the options. If you have presented them with three or four options, you may have anywhere from one to four offers associated with the different deals you have presented. Ask the clients which option works the best for them. Do not make them feel pressured. Let the meeting flow naturally so that they feel comfortable with the situation. Control the timing and try to gently move them to a decision. Provide them with a deadline and show urgency if the clients are not able to make a decision at the meeting.

Meeting with the Funding Source for the Deal

In dealing with the funding source, you will follow many of the same steps as with the client. When you present the deal, offer the funding source several different funding options. Use the same negotiating tactics as discussed earlier to obtain a good deal for your client as well as earn a profit for yourself.

When working a deal, you will need to leave room in the numbers for a reasonable fee for yourself. Work both ends of the deal to your advantage, but do not make either party unhappy. Unhappy customers have a way of coming back to haunt you.

Make sure that you follow any guidelines or restrictions that each particular funding source may have. You should have discovered this information from your investor up front. Make sure you are aware of any surprises on the part of the funding source so that the deal doesn't fall through at the last minute.

As you have seen, negotiating is a lot about listening, building relationships, and developing trust. You can create an atmosphere of cooperation with your clients and help them to solve their problems. You won't be able to help everyone, as some people might already be too far in trouble to even begin to dig out. However, you can enjoy helping the ones you can, and you may find out that the negotiation process is the best part of cash flow investing.

Chapter 9

Goal Setting and Future Success

Creating Success in Your Business

Keeping a positive mindset and setting goals can be key factors in the success of your business. Many of the wealthiest people in America did not inherit their money. They worked hard, and gained and lost money. Some say that many multimillionaires have lost millions over the course of their careers. Because they were willing to take chances that others were not willing to take, it paid off for them in the end.

The last section will talk about things that you can work on to enhance your character and your mindset in business. By improving your inner "self," your professional life will be affected in ways you can only imagine. If you can develop these attributes, you will be successful in business and anything else you do in life.

The "success attributes" that we will discuss will help you to improve yourself and keep your life in balance. You must balance all aspects of your life. If you focus only on your business, then your physical, emotional, and social "self" will be out of balance. Really, take the time to read through these attributes and work on them in your own life. You will find yourself growing as you take each of them into your character.

Challenge and Motivation

Without challenge, people would lack motivation. If everything was easy, then everyone would just go about his or her way, and no one would ever do anything really great. Motivation keeps us going when things get tough and keeps us from quitting.

In your business, people may challenge your right to be in this field. Actually, you may still have doubts about yourself. You must meet these challenges so that you can move forward. First, you must change the way you think. If you do, you will be poised to take advantage of the opportunities to be had in this business. Stop thinking about money in terms of time, or as in dollars per hour; instead, think about it in terms of yourself. Don't think about how much time it will take to close the deal, think only about yourself and the deal. See how you can change your way of thinking?

You must also be willing to find your own challenges to meet your goals. Otherwise, you will lack the motivation to succeed. You must take time to find your passion and make that your personal challenge. If you have a personal challenge or passion, then you can stay motivated at the rough spots when things aren't going so well. Decide what your ultimate goal is. Is it to work from home and spend time with your family? Is it to provide a comfortable retirement for you and your spouse? Is it to stop working for someone else? Find out what it is for YOU, and make that your personal challenge.

Take on the challenge of beginning or moving forward with your business and know that your life will change for the better. Start seeing your current job as a means to an end, something you will stay in only until your new business is supporting you. Start to organize your time differently, and realize the changes that will happen as you enter this exciting new part of your life.

Stay Committed

After you have identified your challenges, the next step is to stay committed to meeting them. You must move from the "just thinking about it" stage into the "I'm doing it today" stage. Become serious about making your business work. Decide to move forward and know that you deserve all the wealth that will flow to you.

If you have trouble committing, take a look at your personal challenge and goals. Perhaps what you thought was your passion, is really something that someone else wants. Make sure it is YOUR passion so that you can commit to it.

Start with general business goals, and then break them down into manageable pieces until you reach your goal. Make sure you write everything down, and don't become overwhelmed. Set "bite-sized" goals that you can handle.

Get Rid of Doubt

The next step before moving toward your goals is to become comfortable with the ideas and goals you have set out for yourself. You need to become comfortable with yourself and your abilities. As you develop your knowledge of the new field, maintain your positive attitude and creativity. It will go a long way toward making you feel comfortable in your new business. Learning from new experiences, remaining professional, and staying comfortable in a deal are things you will eventually need to deal with.

If you are the type of person who doesn't like new things, then just get comfortable with the idea of being uncomfortable. Don't let your doubts and nervousness paralyze you. Eventually, you will find that if you work through your discomfort, you will become used to the feeling and it will eventually go away.

Another way to get rid of your doubts is by learning. If you don't know the answer to something, admit it and assure the person that you will find out the answer. Then take the time to educate yourself. You can also associate with people in your field or find a mentor. Keep a positive attitude, and remember your personal challenge. It will help you to see it all as worthwhile.

Get Organized

The next step in this process is to organize yourself and your business so that it is easy to conduct business. In doing the actual organization of your office, there are certain things you will need to keep your business running smoothly.

- Application packages from factors
- Fax machine
- Phone line dedicated for business only

- Desk
- Filing cabinet
- Business cards
- Marketing materials
- Office supplies
- Web site

Plan your desk and your filing system so it is easy for you to find the worksheets and information you need while on the phone. You want to be able to go right to the correct information while on the phone with a prospective client without fumbling around for paperwork.

Being organized in your office will also help you to keep your mind organized. The more collected you are mentally, the better able you will be to deal with your clients and prospects. Make sure your voice mail or answering machine has a professional message and asks for detailed information. This will better prepare you to handle return calls. Just because you are a "home-based" business, doesn't mean you can stop being professional!

Another way to get organized is to create a business plan. Use your plan to help you meet your goals. If you plan nothing, then nothing will happen. Be reasonable when writing out your plan. You do not want to set yourself up for failure.

Plan blocks of time to make marketing calls, handle paperwork, file documents, exercise, etc. You want to balance all aspects of your life and not allow things to fall through the cracks.

Be Confident

Confidence is defined as self-reliance and boldness, and you will need both qualities to succeed in this field. Do not confuse having confidence with a big ego. Many people are merely cocky, instead of being confident. Don't be pushy or boastful. Let people know how you can help them; don't brag about your accomplishments.

Focus your confidence on what you do and the service you provide instead of on yourself. One reason that keeps most people from feeling confident is a lack of knowledge. Always take the time to study and learn. There is a wealth of information available in libraries, through professional associations, and on the Internet. As you increase your knowledge, you will eventually close a deal. You will see that as you begin to close deals, you feel more confident with each one. The first one is the hardest, but as you find success the first time, your confidence will grow.

Be in Control of Your Business

Are you in control or does your business control you? It is an important factor in your success. Does your business require so much of your time that you have no time left for anything else? You can build in free time and be in control. Don't allow your business building attempts to "drown" you.

Spend your time on the most important things. Prioritize the things you have to do, and then do those things first. Spend 90% of your time finding deals, and the rest will work itself out. Don't make excuses for not getting things done. Plan for time to do the things you need to do. If you have to take your daughter to dance class AND make calls, schedule time to do both. Don't allow your time to control you and use it as an excuse. Careful planning and organization will allow you to do both.

Another facet of control is allowing deals to die that are not going to close, and then moving on to the next one. You can't continue to revive a deal that is dead. Accept that the deal did not work out, or that the client is not serious, and move on. This is being in control of your business.

Establish Credibility

You can establish credibility by having knowledge, knowing how to run a business, and having confidence in yourself. Without credibility, people will not want to do business with you.

You need to maintain a professional image. Be calm and self-possessed when you deal with perspective clients. Credibility does not necessarily mean the number of years you've been in the business. If you have done your research, prepared yourself, and contacted factors, then you can present a professional, credible impression to others. If someone asks how long you've been in business, you can tell the person that you work with people who have been in the business for years.

The most important thing about credibility is for you to feel that you are credible. If you believe it, you will present yourself that way to others. You can lose credibility by being disorganized, flustered, unprofessional, or unprepared. Even during tense moments, if you maintain your professional demeanor instead of falling apart, the client will still believe in your ability to handle the deal.

Your credibility and your reputation go hand in hand, and if you lose credibility in the eyes of a client or potential client, it may come back to haunt you in the form of word of mouth. Conversely, a great reputation can earn you more clients as your former clients recommend you.

Be Willing to Adapt

Marketing professors in colleges have for years given the examples of companies that are not willing to adapt to the changing environment around them. Companies that saw themselves as strictly "railroads" instead of "transportation," or "telephones" instead of "communication" went the way of the dinosaur. These companies were unwilling to ride the changing tides of technology, and, thus, became much more susceptible to "extinction."

Because the financial environment is always changing, you must be willing to adapt and change with it. People who are open to change and to new ideas are the ones who truly succeed because they don't pigeonhole themselves into one small niche.

Change is scary for many people, and it is human nature to shy away from it. But, if you want to be successful, you have got to face your fear and adapt to your business environment. Be willing to change the way you do business in order to close a deal and realize a greater profit.

In order to overcome fear, you first must accept that it is a normal reaction to change. Then realistically look at the outcomes that would follow change. Many times, just evaluating what could happen allows us to make a rational decision because we are not hindered by fear of the unknown.

Establish a Network

Connecting to others is something that will help you both professionally and personally. Networking in the industry will help get your business in front of more people. Networking in your personal and social life keeps you grounded and can also help your business.

Aim to establish professional connections with others in the industry. Contacts such as these can be invaluable in the long run if someone is referring business to you. Maintain and nurture these associations, and return the favor when they send business your way.

Chapter 10

Final Thoughts

I know we've covered a lot and I hope by now you are excited about all things you can do to start a new business or even improve an existing one. Some of what's in this book may come to naturally, other things you may need to learn.

Real estate investing is a great way to make money and it affords a very enjoyable lifestyle. If you pursue some of the techniques and strategies described in this book, you should have enough work to keep you and a couple others busy for at least a few years.

The opportunity potential in real estate investing is much the same whether you are a small home based business or a mega corporation. Some people have started with nothing more than a small idea and turned it into thousand of dollars. Some achieve phenomenal results while others barely break even, and there's good reason why. The most important factors concern desire, commitment, and time management.

No major success happens without desire. Successful people all know what they want and are willing to exert great amounts of energy, effort and money to achieve it. Their eagerness and enthusiasm translates into intense commitment and burning desire. If you want to succeed you must have desire. Work without desire is fruitless and will never get you to where you want to be.

Once you have desire, you must have commitment to that desire. Commitment means that you will persistently forge on until problems are resolved and solutions are found. Desire without commitment doesn't get you anywhere. You need to commit to your desire and turn it into an action plan and then act on that action plan.

The most significant investment in any business is the time you put into it. And like any monetary investment, you want to make sure you invest well, and that means using your time appropriately. Make a list of your immediate short-term goals and plan your days. Proper planning requires systematically thinking about your entire business. Develop a strategy to achieve your goals. The whole point of developing a strategy is to intensely focus on the right things that will achieve results.

I always make a to-do list the night before, and then work through it the next day, crossing things off as I do them. I know it seems trivial, but it feels good to cross things off my list, and motivates me to do the next item on the list.

Instead of starting your day with easy, brainless tasks you don't mind doing, start your day with the hard things that you dislike doing and like to put off. What you usually feel like doing is not usually the highest leverage activity in your business. This way, not only do you get the more difficult tasks completed and off the back of your mind, but it also staves off procrastination.

Furthermore, identify your key areas of profit, and concentrate on spending the bulk of your time, money and effort there. Practice the Pareto Principal. Find the 20% of your business or customers that produce 80% of the profit. Then focus on it. Devote 80% of your efforts to these key areas and leave the remaining 20% for the other things.

Finally and most important, don't expect things to happen overnight. All I can do is give you advice; it's up to you to put in into action. Sit down, set your goals, and get started right away. Don't wait until tomorrow, or the next day to get started. Start right now. The sooner you start, the sooner you can start living the life you want.

You need to act on your thoughts and ideas immediately. Have you ever tuned on the TV or opened a newspaper or magazine and seen someone else making millions with an idea that you had, but never acted on? That could have been you.

The longer it takes you to go from idea to fruition, the less likely you are to complete it and the more likely it is that someone else will.

No matter what you do, always give 110%, 100% of the time. Find your burning desire, commit to that desire then devise an action plan and act on it. Proceed at your own pace. Embrace fear. Embrace life.

Once you make your first million, don't forget to share your newfound wealth with others. Give to charity, tip generously, and most of all believe in yourself. I know you can do it — the only thing stopping you is you.